Praise for *The Gerbil Farmer's Daughter*

"An affectionate tale of domestic life and the frustrations that come with belonging."
—*People* (3½ out of 4 stars)

"In the long parade of memoirs American readers have seen in recent years, have you noticed how few make you laugh out loud? Holly Robinson's book made me laugh so many times my cheeks were a little sore. Her portrait of a little-explored and often-comic landscape, along with the sure and funny narrative voice that is our tour guide through family, gerbils, and love, is one of the best memoirs around. And her prose is sparkling, very particular, and always vivid."
—Susan Straight, National Book Award finalist and author of *A Million Nightingales* and *Highwire Moon*

"Wacky and tender, *The Gerbil Farmer's Daughter* is as much a social history of the 1960s as an intensely personal family memoir. Holly Robinson handles the heavy issues of longing and belonging with wonderful honesty and a light touch." —Stewart O'Nan, author of *Songs for the Missing*

"A delightful memoir about an unusual childhood, complete with a cast of characters led by an eccentric, forward-thinking father and his incredulous, rebellious kids. Think *Cheaper by the Dozen*—but with cute, furry rodents thrown in. I loved it!"
—Sandi Kahn Shelton, author of *A Piece of Normal* and *What Comes After Crazy*

"What a delightful, delicious coming-of-age story—filled with a cast of enchanting, eccentric, utterly memorable characters, and with what is most endearing: the author's affection for them. This is an engrossing tale of family life, and of the extraordinary menagerie that lies at the heart of their adventures. It is as if E. B. White, Gerald Durrell, and Calvin Trillin had conspired to write the funniest, most charming, and most unlikely of tales. Holly Robinson's touch is sure, deft, and loving, and *The Gerbil Farmer's Daughter* is a magical tale that will enthrall children—and readers—of all ages."
—Jay Neugeboren, author of *Imagining Robert* and *The Stolen Jew*

"What does one military man do when he retires from commanding a ship? Why not build the world's largest gerbil farm? Holly Robinson's memoir vividly tells of her life growing up in a military family and of her teenage years as one of the 'employees' in her dad's oddly successful, sometimes exasperating, often humorous livestock venture."

–Douglas Whynott, author of *Following the Bloom* and *A Country Practice*

"Holly Robinson reveals a fascinating, untold chapter in the history of the Mongolian gerbil in the United States as she brings us back to a time before play dates, bike helmets, or other adult meddling in private childhood affairs and tells with vivid clarity of growing up in America in the 1960s into the '70s, all the while struggling to hide a terrible family secret–the barns in the backyard house nine thousand gerbils."

–Donna Anastasi, president of the American Gerbil Society and author of *Gerbils: The Complete Guide to Gerbil Care*

"As improbable as it was that Holly Robinson's crisp and buttoned-down Navy commander of a dad would give it all up for the dream of becoming a gerbil guru, it is not at all surprising that his daughter would craft a memoir that captures his odd and sometimes embarrassing passion so well. Her spirited account is equal parts quirky, funny, heartwarming, and even heartbreaking."

–Madeleine Blais, author of *Uphill Walkers: A Memoir of a Family*

"Robinson writes with humor and honesty, creating a charming story, a reminder of how all the love and care in the world may not be enough, and a moving tribute to a father who, nonetheless, never stopped trying."

–Booklist

"Robinson . . . wryly narrates this memoir about growing up with a stern Navy father who abruptly takes up breeding the then little-known gerbil in the late 1960s . . . interspers[ing] her compelling narrative with accounts of gerbil mayhem."

–Publishers Weekly

"Journalist Robinson cheerfully recalls growing up with a closeted gerbil breeder. . . . It's a scenario that could have been lifted from a 1960s sitcom, but Robinson invests the narrative with pathos, good-natured moments of absurdity, and plenty of keen humor . . . sweet and affecting."

–Kirkus Reviews

The Gerbil Farmer's Daughter

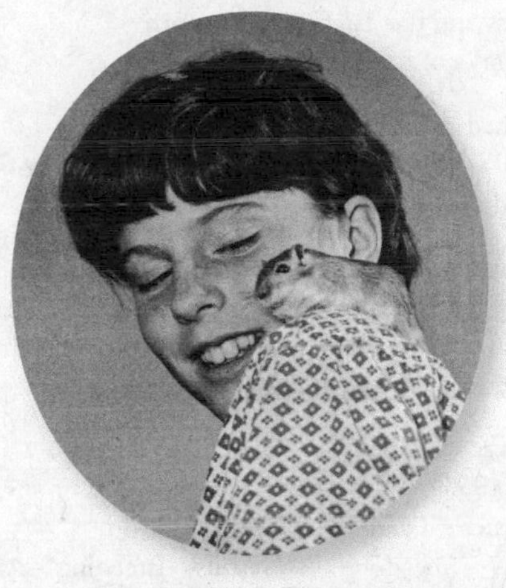

A Memoir

Holly Robinson

THREE RIVERS PRESS • NEW YORK

The names and identifying characteristics of some individuals have been changed to protect their privacy.

Published in the United States by Three Rivers Press,
an imprint of the Crown Publishing Group,
a division of Random House, Inc., New York.
www.crownpublishing.com

Three Rivers Press and the Tugboat design are
registered trademarks of Random House, Inc.

Originally published in hardcover in the United States
by Harmony Books, an imprint of the Crown Publishing Group,
a division of Random House, Inc., New York, in 2009.

Grateful acknowledgement is made to Judith H. Block for permission to reprint the poem "Twilight on the Gobi" by Judith H. Block, copyright © 2003 by Judith H. Block, www.geocities.com/Phoebe_art04.
Reprinted by permission of the author.

Library of Congress Cataloging-in-Publication Data
Robinson, Holly, 1955–
The gerbil farmer's daughter / Holly Robinson.
1. Gerbils as pets—Anecdotes. 2. Gerbils—Breeding—Anecdotes.
3. Robinson, D. G. (Donald Granville), 1928– 4. Robinson,
Holly, 1955– I. Title.
SF459.G4R63 2009
636.935'83—dc22
[B] 2008051449

ISBN 978-0-307-33746-7

Printed in the United States of America

Photographs on title page and page 164 by D. G. Robinson Jr.

DESIGN BY BARBARA STURMAN

10 9 8 7 6 5 4 3 2 1

First Paperback Edition

For my parents and brothers,
who believe, as I do, that being normal is overrated.

And for my husband and children,
who have shown me that passion, friendship, and love
need not be mutually exclusive.

Contents

The Gerbil Farmer's Daughter

Prologue

"That's the one you want?"

My son nods. "It looks like a twig," he says.

Aidan and I are in our favorite pet store, standing in front of a tank of catfish. We come here regularly as a reward after any arduous domestic chore—shoe shopping, food shopping, recycling. It's not one of the new, supersized pet stores, those wannabe Wal-Marts with their broad aisles, gleaming white floors, health foods, and pet accessories that could double as prom jewelry. This store actually sells pets. There are metal bins of squealing guinea pigs that scatter shavings as they stampede into corners. Ferrets lounge like movie stars in hammocks above a cage of solemn lion-faced rabbits, and there's an entire room of fish so dimly lit that it feels like we're swimming underwater, too.

Unlike those cruise ship pet stores, where the sales clerks all seem to be short-tempered men in jobs of last resort after alcohol binges or failed rock-and-roll careers, the clerks here are young and cheerful and tattooed. They have their own flocks of parrots or packs of dogs at home, and they clearly remember being just like Aidan is now: a nine-year-old kid with ant farms, butterfly nets, animal traps, fishing rods, and a zeal for dissecting owl pellets. Aidan even has a nifty bug vacuum that sucks insects out of tree bark. Because of him, we have two dogs, two cats, two tanks of fish, and two hamsters; it's a lot like living with Noah without the ark.

"This is a *Farlowella* catfish," the skinny blond clerk murmurs as she nets one of the wriggling, whiskered twigs and drops it into a plastic bag filled with water. "It won't give your tetras any trouble," she promises Aidan. "They're not nippy like other catfish."

Aidan is right at her elbow, nearly dancing in place with excitement. When he grows up, he wants to be either a cave explorer or an inventor; either way, he will live in the woods and trap his own animals as pets. He plans to build his house by hand, and his furniture, too. I believe him.

As we make our way into the brightly lit main room of the pet store, Aidan takes my hand and tugs me toward the rodent room. "We have to see Screamer before we go," he reminds me.

The clerk laughs and leaves our new algae eater adrift in its own private plastic bubble next to the cash register. Then she leads us over to the cages of rats and mice and hamsters, where the white mice are on top of the exercise wheel instead of inside it, tumbling off and then climbing right back on again.

Screamer is in the glass tank above the mice. He's the most famous hamster we know, so famous that he's not even for sale. This is because, although he is small and brown and short-haired like most hamsters, he screams every time someone picks him up and turns him onto his back. It's an ungodly noise, hissing and shrill at the same time, like the cranky water pipes I once had in a San Francisco apartment.

The clerk tips the hamster upside down, and Screamer's cries drill through my skull. Then the girl flips the hamster over again and tucks him back into his nest. In the sudden silence, Aidan notices a new tank of animals next to Screamer's.

"What are those?" he asks, pushing his face close to the glass. "They're not hamsters."

"They're gerbils," I tell him. "They're good pets because they don't use much water, so their cages don't smell as bad as your hamster cage. They don't eat their babies, either, like hamsters do sometimes."

Aidan looks up at me and blinks in surprise. "How do you know so much about gerbils, Mom?"

I bite my lip and consider dodging the question. Our five children know all about their grandfather's career as a Navy officer. That always seemed like enough family lore to take to elementary school: a grandpa who left his boyhood home in Ohio to go to the U.S. Naval Academy and serve his country for twenty years, first in the Korean War, then as the captain of a ship that transported tanks and Marines, and finally as head of naval science at the Merchant Marine Academy on Long Island. We have my dad's oil portrait to prove it. The painting, which always hung in my parents' front hall, shows Dad in uniform, his eyes blue and far-gazing, his shoulders square, his features chiseled and handsome beneath the gold-braided cap. He looks like President Gerald Ford on steroids. There is no hint in that portrait of who my dad really is.

Clearly, the way to approach this conversation with Aidan

is nonchalantly, as if I were dispensing some routine edicts from the adult world, the way I answer his questions about sex or why voting matters. Nothing flashy. Just the facts.

"Your grandfather used to raise gerbils," I tell Aidan casually as we pay for the catfish and start walking toward the car. "I thought I told you that."

This tactic fails. Aidan looks stunned. As well he should: Aidan only knows my father as a quiet, bald retiree whose favorite activities are reading and Scrabble, so the idea of my father raising gerbils is outrageous to him. I might as well have confessed that my dad was a Broadway dancer.

"No," Aidan says.

"Oh. Well, he did," I assure him as I unlock the car and hand the catfish to Aidan in the backseat. "We had a lot of gerbils at one time."

"Like a whole cageful?" Aidan asks doubtfully.

I put the key in the ignition and turn it. "More."

"How many more?"

I don't want to talk about this. I've never talked about my father's other life. As my brother Donald always says, "Telling people about Dad just makes them ask more questions." But Aidan, of all my children, deserves to know, because there is no child more like my father than this one. "We had thousands more," I tell him as we head home. "Like, nine thousand gerbils."

When I glance at Aidan in the rearview mirror, he is frowning hard. It is the same expression he has when we talk about the tooth fairy: my youngest son wants to believe, because he likes finding dollar bills under his pillow. But he doesn't want to be the only kid in school whose parents can trick him. "You're kidding me, right, Mom?"

"Nope."

"Where did Grandfather keep them?" Aidan challenges. "In the garage?"

"At first," I admit. "And then the gerbils were in our basement, and then he built buildings for them. Big buildings. We had a gerbil farm."

"Mom," Aidan says excitedly, "was Grandfather in the *Guinness Book of World Records*?"

I laugh. "No. But he could have been, I bet. He raised more gerbils than anyone else in the world."

"Wow," Aidan says with a sigh. "But why, Mom?"

By now, we are nearly home. And it's a good thing, too, because that's one question that has no easy answer.

Chapter One

Mail-Order Gerbils

Don't squeeze!

CREDIT: D. G. ROBINSON JR.

One cloudy Monday afternoon,

I came home and found my family gathered in the garage. I'd been pedaling my bike around the neighborhood after school, pretending that the bike was a horse I was racing around the cul-de-sacs. I'd ridden so hard through the soupy Virginia heat that my short bangs were glued to my forehead and my knobby knees were shaking as I dismounted the bike and walked it up the driveway.

My brother Donald raced outside when he saw me. Donald was eight years old, skinny and quick and so blond that he looked bald in most lights. It didn't help his looks any that Mom buzzed his hair like a Marine's, which only called attention to the fact that Donald's head was so long and narrow that everyone, even our parents, called him Picklehead.

"Dad got boxes from Air Express," Donald said. "Now he's opening them!"

I dropped my books and lunchbox down on the cement floor of the garage and went to stand between Donald and my mother, who carried my little sister, Gail. We stood close together in the dim oily cave of the garage and watched in silence while my father—a methodical man who never went anywhere without a list, a map, and a pocketknife—unpacked the boxes with his usual precision.

As Dad slid out the contents of that first box with the help of a metal ruler, I saw that it was a plastic cage with a wire top. The wire top had two dips in it, one for a water bottle and the other for food. Dad held the cage high up like a holy chalice to admire its contents. Through the opaque bottom of the cage, I could make out two dark, round shadows that skittered this way and that. My mouth went dry with excitement.

"What do you think of them, Sally?" Dad asked.

Mom wrinkled her nose. My mother was thirty-two years old that summer, but she often dressed in shorts that showed off her figure and tied bright scarves over her short brown curls. She was girlish and lovely, like Elizabeth Taylor in *National Velvet,* but without the scary violet eyes. "They look like rats to me," she said. "Look at those awful tails."

"What are they, Dad?" Donald asked.

"Gerbils."

There were four cages in all, in four separate Air Express boxes. The process of meticulously unpacking the boxes and examining their contents took Dad so long that by the time he'd lined the cages up on the metal shelves installed along the back wall of the garage, Donald and I were giving each other Indian burns and Mom was on her third cigarette.

At last, though, the gerbil cages were on the shelves and I was able to stand on tiptoe to peer into them. Each plastic bin held a pair of palm-sized animals with long tails. The tails had tiny black tufts at the ends, like miniature lion tails. The gerbils were a warm sand color with creamy underbellies and shiny black eyes; their eyes looked just like the buttons our grandmother Keach sewed onto sock monkeys for her gift shop in Maine. I wanted to put a gerbil on my bed and kiss it.

"Where did you get them?" I asked.

Dad handed me a catalog from inside one of the boxes. It was Creative Playthings, a toy catalog that Donald and I routinely fought over until we reduced it to confetti, even though we knew that Dad would never buy us anything from a catalog except school clothes from Sears. The gerbils were advertised in the "Discovering Nature" section for $5.50 a pair, a fortune.

Donald yanked the catalog out of my hands and asked Dad why he hadn't gotten the Tom Thumb greenhouse or the egg incubator, too. I pushed my face close to the plastic side of one cage. The gerbils inside it surprised me by bounding around on their hind legs like tiny, caffeinated kangaroos.

"Can I hold one?" I asked, tugging on the pocket of Dad's khaki uniform pants. He had taken off his brass-buttoned Navy shirt with the bars and stripes, but the pants were still cinched tight around his white undershirt with a shiny black belt that matched his shiny black shoes. You could see your face in those shoes.

"Not yet," he said. "Let them get used to us."

We left the gerbils and went inside to have supper and watch TV, all of us oblivious to the fact that Dad, with one whimsical purchase from a toy catalog, had charted a new course for our family's future.

WINTER must come to Virginia, but in my memory Virginia was always hot. It wasn't the sort of sunny hot that you'd want to bask in, either, but the sticky sort of hot that makes your skin feel like it's melting off your bones. If there was ever a breeze, it stank of dead crab and rotting marsh grasses, and the lawns were hopping with chiggers and ticks and fleas.

A few months before the gerbils arrived, we had moved to Virginia Beach from Annapolis, Maryland, where my father was teaching at the Naval Academy before becoming captain of the USS *Grant County,* LST 1174. We lived in a housing development of uninspired brick ranch houses with minimalist landscaping, shiny avocado appliances, sunken living rooms, and long hallways perfect for sliding races in your socks. Southern Point jutted into Wolfsnare Lake like the thumb of a mitten; I suppose the mucky smells must have been the result of living not on a real lake but beside a glorified swamp created by damming up a piece of the Chesapeake Bay. All around us, new houses were going up so fast that we were surrounded by wooden skeletons.

Still, as bad as it was outside, it was better than being in school. There were more than thirty kids in my fifth-grade class and most were Navy, with fathers stationed at Naval Station Norfolk or Naval Air Station Oceana. Like me, they'd lived in different countries and different states, and had moved every year or two with their families. School, for us, was always a place where we had to reinvent ourselves, a parade ground where you had a chance to show your colors.

One boy managed to set fire to a trash can every day. The ceiling was covered with so many sticky paper spit cones that it was like sitting in a cave thick with stalactites. One of the girls frequently climbed outside and stood on the second-floor window ledge until the teacher next door noticed her face at the window and came running over, her dress damp with sweat beneath her armpits.

I was not a bad kid, nor an especially good one. I chose to remain invisible. I spent most of my school days reading horse stories inside my textbooks and pretending I was breaking mustangs in Wyoming or running with the wild ponies of Chincoteague, while at the same time wishing for a friend. So far, the only person who spoke to me with any regularity was the school bus driver, a skinny old man whose breath smelled of coffee and bacon, and who tucked my school picture into his bus visor as part of his collection of carefully combed children.

Since I had no friends, the gerbils provided a welcome distraction. After school I'd go right into the garage and sit on a stepladder in the relative cool, breathing in the heady scents of motor oil, pine shavings, and the slightly musky odor of desert animals. Gerbils were far more entertaining to watch than my brother's ill-tempered hamster, which remained curled in a tight fist of fur all day and reared up to bite if you tried to stroke it with a finger. Gerbils didn't sleep during daylight hours, but scurried and bounded and sniffed with great purpose. They thumped their long back feet when frightened or sat up on their hind legs to stare at me with their black button eyes. (I suppose I served the same purpose for them as they did for me.) The gerbils were frantic diggers, too, constantly clawing at the corners of their cages as if certain that an entire maze of freedom tunnels lay just out of paw's reach.

The gerbils seemed to cheer my father up. Dad went to his ship every day the way TV dads went to their offices, and the stress of his new post as the commanding officer of a ship had made him humorless and stern, like the despot of a small, unimportant country. Now, instead of sitting at the dinner table with his cigarette and sighing with his head in his hands, as he'd done nearly every night since our arrival in Virginia, he put on old clothes and went straight out to the garage to tend his new livestock. The gerbils ate little and drank even less, so there wasn't much to do, but Dad kept a gerbil journal and jotted down his observations.

On Saturdays, my father let me fill the water bottles for the gerbils and drop handfuls of green pellets onto their cage lids. But no matter how many times I asked if I could hold a gerbil, he said no. "These aren't your pets," he said. "Not like Donald's hamster or your guinea pig. These are my pets, and I just want to watch them."

"Can't I at least show them to my friends?" I asked. I didn't have any friends yet, but I was certain that showing off our gerbils could get me some. A gerbil was much better than those miniature dogs and monkeys advertised in comic books, always photographed in silly teacups. And there was just no comparison between a gerbil and a sea monkey. Sea monkey ads showed grinning creatures costumed in tiny dresses and suits, but anybody who'd ever been tricked into buying them knew that sea monkeys were only ant-sized brine shrimp that arrived as dried eggs in tiny envelopes.

But my father would not relent. "Don't you dare touch my gerbils," he said. "And don't you let anyone near the garage, either. Those are strict orders."

"Yes, sir, Daddy, sir," I said.

When my father looked straight at you with his blue eyes, you had to say that. You also had to square your shoulders and lift your chin, the same way the sailors and Marines looked at Dad when they were saluting.

My father was six feet tall, thin and muscular and handsome. The year we moved to Virginia, he was only thirty-five years old but already nearly bald, a fact that he claimed was due to us kids making such a racket that he couldn't even hear himself think, so how could we expect his poor hair to grow?

At home, Dad liked to be our captain just as he was captain on his ship. To prove his point, he sometimes made us eat "square meals" like he ate when he was at the Naval Academy. "It's good discipline for plebes," he'd tell us as we lifted our forks straight up and moved them at right angles to our mouths, dropping food along the way, especially Jell-O with Cool Whip, Mom's favorite new easy family dessert.

Also, before we left the dinner table, we were expected to say, "May we please be excused from the table, Daddy, sir?" and wait for him to say, "Permission granted, plebes."

Now Dad ordered me to keep the garage door shut good and tight, too. "The neighbors don't need to know our business."

Later, when I asked Mom why the gerbils were so top-secret, she sighed. "Raising gerbils in your garage is very un-Navy behavior," she explained. "Just do as your father says."

"But doesn't it bother you when Dad goes out to the garage every night after dinner?" I asked.

"Not really." Mom shrugged. "Some men have golf. Mine has gerbils."

~

No matter how closely I watched them, I could never be sure when the gerbils were having sex. One would jump on top of another and there would be a scramble, but that could as likely happen in a cage of young males vying for leadership as it could between a breeding pair in the mood for love. I just knew that the gerbils were making babies. Within a month, all but one of Dad's original pairs had a litter; within two months, they'd bred again and Dad was setting up cages for new pairs out of the first litters.

Telling the difference between male and female gerbils was easy, Dad said. One Saturday, while I was helping him fill water bottles, he held a pair of gerbils up by their tails to show me how the females had two touching buttons and the males had theirs separated with a bulge to either side. It didn't seem to matter which one you picked as a mate for any particular gerbil, either; any couple would happily make a nest together.

What would make a Navy officer sitting on a ship in the middle of the Mediterranean Sea consider raising gerbils in his garage? By late spring, when the shelves along the back wall of our garage were half filled with cages, it finally occurred to me to wonder.

"Why do you want so many gerbils, Dad?" I asked one morning as I helped wash his car, taking care to scrub dirt off the wheel wells with a toothbrush just as he'd shown me. My father cared for his cars the way he cared for his ship: everything had to be spit-shined and tuned up and sparkling. Unfortunately for his family, we were his only crew.

"Oh, I don't know," he said absently. "I might sell some as pets, or maybe write a book about them. You know, I can't find a thing about gerbils in the library."

I reported this exciting news to my mother later. She was in the kitchen with her mother, Maybelle Keach, and she was not impressed. Mom was such an animal lover that we'd had pet mice, turtles, rabbits, guinea pigs, hamsters, dogs, cats, and even lizards through the years. Yet she still couldn't find room in her heart for gerbils.

"It's those damn rat tails," she told me. "I just can't overlook those tails."

My mother had graduated from the University of Maine with a degree in Romance languages and was offered jobs with the UN as an interpreter and at Pan Am as a flight attendant, but she'd chosen my father instead. She was determined to make a go of being a wife and mother and threw herself into every domestic task with an overabundance of energy and intelligence.

At the start of our lives in Virginia, she had gone on an antiquing kick, painting our furniture Colonial blue and then streaking it black. On the morning that I spelled out Dad's plans for writing a book about gerbils, hopping from one foot to the other in my excitement, Mom was engaged in a brand-new hobby: decoupage. Each day, another piece of furniture in our house was graced with a magazine picture shellacked to its surface.

"Honest to God," Mom said, and began to furiously slap a fresh coat of varnish onto an end table, where she'd glued a picture of pink roses in a white pitcher. "What will that man think of next? This is one little hobby that I wish he'd outgrow in a hurry."

Grandmother beckoned me over to the kitchen table and made me sit down. She was peeling potatoes for dinner, and it was high time I learned how, she said. "At your age, I was fixing dinner for my entire family."

Grandmother had sold her gift shop and moved from Maine to Virginia to be closer to us, and she was trying hard to help Mom raise us "the way we should be raised." She was British and was always dressed for an outing, in case the opportunity arose. She was fond of reminding us that her father had once guarded Queen Victoria's jewels. That day, she wore a cotton button-down green shirtdress with a white belt. Her hair, as always, was freshly curled and, as she'd told me once in a fit of pride, "Titian red." Despite her careful appearance, though, she was always doing something useful, usually in the kitchen. Her potato skins came off in a single swirl of peel, like brown ribbons unraveling into the white ceramic bowl. My own were more like fingernail cuttings.

Grandmother kept a close eye on my peeling progress while she addressed my mother. "You never can tell, Sally," Grandmother said. "It's possible that Robbie could make some pocket money with the gerbils." She and my mother were the only ones who still called my dad "Robbie," a nickname he'd earned for his last name, Robinson, during his Annapolis days.

"I can't imagine that gerbils will ever be much of a craze," Mom said. "Look at them! And they're eating us out of house and home."

"Has he sold any at all?" Grandmother asked.

"Oh, a few here and there to pet stores. But you heard Holly. Now he's talking about writing a book!" Mom shook her head. "A book! Who in his right mind would ever want to read a book about gerbils?"

Grandmother said, "Well, just you be grateful that gerbils aren't chickens. We had hundreds of chickens when you were growing up, Sally, remember? All of them flapping and clucking and crowing until I thought I'd go out of my mind."

"Of course you have to defend the gerbils," Mom sniffed. "It's all your fault that we have them. If you hadn't shown Robbie that damn article about gerbils in *Newsweek,* I wouldn't have a bunch of Mongolian pocket kangaroos living in my garage."

"The gerbils are quiet, though," Grandmother reminded her. "You don't even know they're in the garage. Be glad of that, Sally."

~

IT WAS true that buying gerbils was really Grandmother Maybelle's idea. She'd come across an article about gerbils in the December 27, 1965, issue of *Newsweek* magazine and showed it to Dad. "I thought the kids might like these," she told him.

Later, after our first pairs of gerbils were installed in the garage, I asked Dad if I could see the article. The brief feature, "Here Come the Gerbils," began by asking, "Will Mongolian gerbils take over the world? The long-tailed bright-eyed rodents may weigh less than 3 ounces, but they are off to a good start. This Christmas the gerbils . . . are already challenging hamsters as the favored pet."

According to that article, Creative Playthings president Frank Caplan had initially offered gerbils for sale "as a jest" and was amazed by the response. Gerbils apparently started to fly off the shelves the minute he advertised them.

"We had to tell the breeder to work overtime for Christmas," Caplan is quoted as saying, despite the gerbil's "slight resemblance to the mouse-rat family," an unfortunate association that he admitted "may prejudice some mothers" against them, as it had mine.

It would be inaccurate to say that my father read that article and saw an easy buck in gerbils. More to the point, he was fascinated by them, and knew this would be a self-sustaining hobby if he could breed the gerbils and sell them to pet stores.

And breed they did. Our Virginia garage seemed to be the perfect gerbil hothouse, with new litters appearing every four weeks. Soon we had nearly two hundred gerbils.

I'd never seen anything being born before, so I loved to watch the babies appear. Most gerbil mothers had four to six babies, but sometimes they'd surprise me and have only one or up to ten. The birthing mothers would race around the cage, seemingly frantic. Then they'd suddenly freeze in place, a look of absolute concentration on their faces as a baby emerged, pink and blind and squirming. It was like the most amazing magic trick in the world. Or like spring: one minute there was only dirt, and the next you'd see a purple crocus.

Once in a while, a mother would help the birth along by reaching between her hind legs to pull out the pup with her paws or teeth. Then she'd eat the goo surrounding the baby, a process that made me nearly gag but fascinated me anyway.

Certain gerbil moms delivered their pups in a tidy pile,

while others dashed madly around the cage as if being chased, dropping babies all over creation. Then, when it was over, these mothers would resolutely dig their babies out of the shavings and drag them over to a nest, usually in a corner, where the babies would peep like newly hatched chicks. The disconsolate fathers watched this process from a distance and slept alone for a few days, but otherwise seemed unbothered by parenthood.

As I watched the pups wiggle around in search of their mother's milk, I couldn't help but compare them to my sister, Gail. She had arrived in our lives just as red-faced and bald and squinty as a gerbil pup. My mother must have given birth to all of us, I reasoned, though I couldn't imagine Mom pulling off that goo with her teeth. Now I wondered why she hadn't nursed Gail.

Finally I asked. "Mom, couldn't you have fed Gail yourself, instead of giving her bottles?"

Mom was frying hamburger patties, which she'd serve with mashed potatoes and a nice thick gravy of Campbell's cream of mushroom soup. She rolled her eyes at me from her post by the stove.

"You've been reading too many books about Africa," she said. "You can try that with your own babies if you want, but I prefer to think of myself as civilized."

Chapter Two

The Gerbil Whisperer

Aboard our cabin cruiser

Part of being a successful mother, as Mom saw it, was to raise independent children. She was a strong proponent of the idea that children should amuse themselves, so unless we were stuffed into the back of the car for family trips, where we rattled about like loose change, we were blissfully free of parental supervision even when we might have preferred their company.

Just before our move to Virginia, for instance, Dad had kept a cabin cruiser on Chesapeake Bay. At cocktail hour, our parents would strap Donald and me into life jackets, hitch us onto ropes, and drop us into the water. They made sure to hoist up the ladder as we paddled and bobbed like bright orange ducklings around the boat. I was happy enough, but scrawny Donald was miserably blue-lipped with cold in minutes. He'd mewl at Mom to let down the ladder, but she'd lean over the boat railing to gaze down at him with a drink in one hand and a cigarette in the other, shaking her head.

"Just a few more minutes, kids," she'd say. "Your father and I need some time to ourselves."

One day, when I complained about being friendless in our new Virginia neighborhood, Mom told me to stop moping.

"Moping never helped anything. You know it'll all be better before you're married. Find something to do. Go watch TV or read a book."

I'd lost interest in television. Dad hadn't wanted to pay for a color set like our neighbor's, so he'd bought a $2 strip of tricolored plastic. The colors on the plastic sheet ran in strips, with green on the bottom, pink in the middle, and blue along the top.

"There," he'd announced. "Color TV without the cost."

Mom wasn't convinced. "I don't know. Everyone has pink eyes," she pointed out. "They look like albinos."

Trying to follow the action of the Lone Ranger through the blurred edges of the color strips made me seasick, so I stopped watching television completely and read more than ever. Every home movie of me in Virginia starts with me reading in a corner until a big pair of adult hands grabs the book away and I'm forced to look up at the camera, blinking and tipping my head like a startled chicken.

As spring edged toward summer, however, I finally found a friend of my own. Marcy Cahill and I met when we were both forced into Girl Scouts. My mother was an overzealous troop leader who led us on sweaty hikes through the Norfolk Botanical Garden and invited a "hygiene lady" to our meeting to explain why it was essential for girls "to wipe from front to back, always front to back, following urination," until Marcy and I about peed right in the kitchen from laughing.

Marcy and I fit together like bookends. Both of us were readers and animal lovers and *Star Trek* fans, to the point where we dressed in identical blue jeans and red turtlenecks to look like crew members of the starship *Enterprise*. This behavior did little to enhance our popularity at school, but we went ahead and built our own starship *Enterprise* out of cardboard boxes in Marcy's garage.

Because Marcy was my best friend, I knew I had to show her the gerbils. After all, Marcy and I had cut our fingers and rubbed our blood together to be sisters after a Girl Scout sleepover, the morning after discovering that the other girls had dipped our underpants in water and frozen them in the camp freezer. I just had to wait until the right moment, when Dad was at sea and wouldn't know I'd disobeyed orders.

As it turned out, though, I didn't wait that long. One May morning, Marcy and I decided to marry my guinea pig, George, to Marcy's rabbit in my backyard. We had to struggle to get George into the bow tie I had made for him out of one of Mom's red checked dish towels. Marcy's rabbit was already white as a bride, so all we had to do was weave a dandelion crown and hang it over her ears. This would've been easier if her ears hadn't already been pasted flat to her head, the result of our fox terrier, Tip, barking so hard at us from his chain that he was hopping up and down as if he were being stung by bees. Tip's biggest goal in life was to swallow another animal whole.

Dad was outside with us. My father never sat still. Every night, after watching the news about Vietnam, he would burn up excess energy by conducting booming, fierce military marches he played on the hi-fi, using his Camel cigarette as a baton. He also made good use of his workshop. In addition to building a pair of miniature pine thrones for either side of the fireplace, he'd found a giant cable spool by the side of the road and somehow got it home, where he sanded it, varnished it, and then rolled it into the house with a thundering sound on the wood floors that made Tip bark and Gail cry. We used the spool as a coffee table, even though Mom complained that it was like having a redwood growing in the den.

Since spring, Dad had spent his free time outdoors, first building a screened-in porch and then turning his attention to landscaping. Our backyard resembled a miniature forest because of the tiny trees Dad had planted everywhere, most of them willows and poplars. The white paint on those skinny trunks made it seem like we were growing a crop of canes for the blind. Now he was digging another hole.

Marcy, whose father outranked mine and who had a teenage sister who sat out in the yard and smoked marijuana for all the world to see, wasn't the least bit afraid of my father. Never mind that Dad, if he wasn't actually issuing orders to us or informing us of something, was prone to such long silences that it was like he didn't see you at all. Marcy stood up, leaving her rabbit in my lap with George, and walked right over to him.

"What in Sam Hill are you doing, Commander Robinson?" Marcy asked, standing with one hand on her hip like she was already a grown-up, even though the backside of her shorts was covered with grass stains and her white anklets had half disappeared into her sneakers.

My father, unaccustomed to being interrupted, did not pause in his digging to correct her language. However, because Marcy's dad outranked him, he did answer her. "Whatever do you mean, Marcy?"

"Why are you planting all these trees?" she demanded.

Dad shrugged and continued to dig. "Somebody will

move into this house when we move out, right?" he asked her. "And don't you think they'd enjoy a little more shade than we've got?"

"Yes, sir."

Dad nodded, but it was as if he were nodding to himself, because he still didn't look at Marcy. "I guess you might say I'm planting for the future, then," he said. This phrase seemed to please him, because he lit another cigarette and then started digging harder, as if his white T-shirt weren't already see-through with sweat.

Marcy traipsed back over to me, her short black hair so straight and stiff, the edges of it stroked her jaw on both sides like paintbrushes. "Your dad is crazy," she said admiringly. "Just plain crazy."

I took a deep breath, encouraged by my best friend's daring. "He has a secret, too," I whispered as Dad pushed the wheelbarrow with its lone occupant, a sapling the size of my arm, down toward the lakeshore. "Come on. I'll show you, but you have to swear not to tell anyone."

I led Marcy by the hand to the side door of the garage. She was carrying her rabbit and I held my guinea pig on his back like a baby in my arms, so getting the door open was tricky. I finally managed to push it open. We slipped into the cool garage and I closed the door immediately behind us. I stopped and blinked in the sudden dark, and we both stood perfectly still for several moments to keep from walking into things.

"What's that scratching sound?" Marcy whispered.

"My dad's new pets," I whispered back. We edged around our turquoise Buick toward the back of the garage. My eyes were getting used to the light, which mainly came from the two windows in the garage door, a pair of dusty slits.

When we reached the metal shelves that now ran along the back and both sides of the garage, I flicked on the light so that Marcy could see the towers of gerbil cages. I fervently hoped that Dad wouldn't suddenly come around to the front of the house and realize the light was on. I was disobeying orders for sure.

Marcy's dark eyes went wide. "What are they?" she asked.

"Shhh. Whisper," I reminded her. "They're gerbils from Mongolia. Gerbils are a kind of kangaroo rat that lives in the desert. Dad calls them pocket kangaroos because they can jump."

We stood in silence as the animals went about their business. Every so often, a gerbil would bound around, knocking against the sides of its cage, or a baby would squeak. By now, Marcy was making little panting noises of excitement, like our fox terrier when he saw the gerbils.

I knew one more trick. "Watch this," I said, and clapped my hands smartly together. The sound startled George the guinea pig—he squealed, and I almost dropped him. Marcy's rabbit thumped her feet, so Marcy had to hang on to her by the scruff of her neck. But it was worth it: in the dim light, I could see that the gerbils had all frozen upright on their hind legs, heads turned toward us as if we were the movie and they were the audience.

~

ONE Saturday morning, Dad went off to the Sears, Roebuck in Virginia Beach to buy tools, an odyssey that could take all day. My mother was inside, coloring with Gail, and Donald had done his usual disappearing act after breakfast, probably off to torment the construction workers or hunt for turtles along the marshy lakeshore.

I slipped into the garage and lifted one edge of the metal lid off the cage of female gerbils I'd been studying for the past week. I didn't remove the lid completely, for fear the animals might escape. Instead, I slid my arm into the cage and lay my hand flat on the bottom of the cage, palm up. With my free hand, I reached into my pocket to extract the sunflower seeds I'd taken from my brother's box of hamster food. I lined my palm with the seeds.

This group of gerbils was nearly full-grown by now, and there was one in particular that I liked because she had a crooked tail like my grandmother's Siamese cat. I'd named her Kinky, and now I called her to me. "Here, Kinky, Kinky, Kinky," I whispered.

Kinky and her sisters ran over to my hand, probably more in response to the alien sight and smell than to my voice, but I liked to imagine that Kinky knew her name right away. Tiny claws tickled my palm as the gerbils sat on my hand and went after the seeds. They didn't store seeds in their cheeks the way Donald's hamster did, but ate them on the spot. In no time, the seeds were gone, and before I could remove my hand, Kinky had climbed right up my arm. She was nearly out of the cage before I shook her off.

The gerbil landed on her back but was unhurt. She immediately scrambled to her feet and sat up on her hind legs, watching me to see what would happen next. "Sorry," I apologized, and repeated the whole process of sliding my hand into the cage and dropping a few seeds into my open palm.

It took me two weeks to fully train Kinky. By the time I was finished, I could coax her to climb right up my arm and down my shoulder to search for seeds in my shirt pocket, and I could hold her in the palm of my hand and feed her sunflowers from my lips. She would ride comfortably in my pocket, too, just her little head sticking up to observe her passing surroundings. I'd ferry Kinky in this way from the garage to my bedroom, where I'd let her rampage through my stable of plastic horse statues and sit in my Barbie car.

Eventually, I felt comfortable enough to ride my bike to Marcy's house with Kinky in my pocket so that she could join our *Star Trek* games. We were deep in one such game—I was playing Mr. Spock and using the Vulcan technique of joining two minds to communicate with Kinky by pressing my forehead to hers—when we were interrupted.

"Girls." Marcy's mother was a slim figure silhouetted in the relentless afternoon sunshine beyond the garage. "Holly has to go home right away. Her mother needs her."

Stunned, I pedaled home as fast as I could without spilling my gerbil. What could possibly be wrong that Mom would call me home in the middle of a perfectly good Saturday morning? On most Saturdays, Donald and I came home only if we were hungry or it was dark, and sometimes not even then.

My mouth went dry and I leaned forward over the handlebars, though not so far that Kinky could leap out of my pocket. What if something had happened to someone in my family? I also had more selfish concerns: What if Dad had discovered that Kinky was missing, and knew I'd disobeyed his orders not to touch the gerbils? Or what if he saw Kinky in my pocket when I rode up the driveway?

As it turned out, I had plenty of time to slip Kinky back into the cage with her sisters. The garage was empty, the big front doors securely shut as usual. I dropped Kinky back into her cage. Then I retraced my steps through the garage and entered the house by the front door.

I found Mom in the backyard. She stood on the lawn next to the lake, where Dad was dragging Gail's empty bright blue plastic wading pool across the lawn. "Oh, good, you're here," Mom said.

She held me by the shoulders and looked me up and down, then sent me back inside for a clean blouse. "Wear the red striped one," she called after me. "I ironed it and hung it up in your closet. Put on a clean pair of shorts and comb your hair, too."

This was getting more mysterious by the minute. By the time I returned to the yard Donald was there, too, in an equally stiff shirt, hair combed and slicked to one side, only his sly blue eyes a clue to his real nature.

Unlike me, Donald had no interest in reading. In fact, he hated any sort of calm. As my mother put it, "Poor little Donald needs more action than he gets." We lived on a lake, and my brother loved to mix himself a tall glass of chocolate milk for breakfast at 5:00 A.M. before sneaking outside to catch frogs and snakes beneath the dock. He was a petty thief who would try every back door until he could get into a neighbor's kitchen and help himself to food better than ours. He lifted restaurant tips so fast that waitresses went home shortchanged while

Donald always had enough money for Cokes. He even swiped coins from the collection plate at the Lutheran church where Mom sent him alone to Sunday school; we weren't Lutherans, but Mom sent him anyway, hoping that "somebody over there will save that kid's soul."

Donald had a genius for escaping mischief unscathed, which left me as his fall guy. Arguing with Donald was like arguing with a prophet: he always knew he was right. During the short time we'd lived in Virginia, he had already convinced me to lick a frozen pipe and race a newspaper boy on a bicycle, which led to me being run over by the bicycle and breaking my nose. Most recently, Donald had convinced me to climb to the top of a telephone pole, using the same metal rungs the telephone repairmen used, and shimmy down it again in shorts; Mom had to spend an entire evening plucking splinters out of my legs.

My mother came up to me as I stood there waging war with Donald. She whipped a comb out of her apron pocket and dragged it through my short hair with a heavy, hopeless sigh. My hair was as dry and brown as toast; Mom had to spit on the comb to make the strands lie down. Then she ordered me to stand next to Donald until our father was ready.

"Ready for what?" I asked, but Mom ignored this and went to sit in the shade with two-year-old Gail, who was dressed in a ruffled blouse. With that outfit and her wild blond curls tamed into ringlets, Gail looked like somebody's princess doll.

Donald sidled closer to me as we watched Dad drag the wading pool to first one location, then another, with Tip the fox terrier barking madly at the scraping sound. "You're stupid," Donald said, and hammered his fist into my thigh.

"Not as stupid as you," I said automatically, punching him back. It was our standard greeting.

Donald grabbed my arm and pinched it hard. Before I could pinch him back, Dad ordered us to collect toys from our bedrooms and bring them outside. "Anything small," he added. He was dressed in a white T-shirt and baggy khaki shorts, his pale legs sticking out like straws. A cigarette hung from one corner of his mouth. "Make it quick, before the light changes."

Donald, Gail, and I ran through the house as if we were on a treasure hunt. I gathered dolls, plastic horse statues, and stuffed animals. When I brought out my armload of belongings to the yard, Dad commanded me to dump everything on the grass near the wading pool. Donald and Gail did the same.

Dad selected a few items and began arranging them in the swimming pool, standing back every now and then to squint at his handiwork like an artist with a canvas. Once satisfied, he went into the garage. He returned with one of the gerbil cages and a black leather case.

Dad lifted a gerbil out of the cage by its tail and dropped it into the wading pool. The animal fell with a plop and froze for a moment, stunned. Then the gerbil began darting through the toys, climbing blocks, digging under stuffed animals, and sitting up on its hind legs to examine one of the plastic horses.

"Okay, kids. Gather around the pool and look interested," Dad commanded.

He moved us closer together. When we were positioned shoulder to shoulder, kneeling beside the wading pool, he lifted a camera out of the black bag beside him.

"Try to smile, kids," Mom encouraged, lighting another

cigarette from her perch on the shady back stoop. She'd poured herself a glass of iced tea, too, so that she could fully enjoy the show.

For the next few hours, we modeled with gerbils. Every now and then Dad would return the gerbil in the wading pool to its cage and pluck a fresh animal out to drop in its place. I wondered if, to the gerbils, it was like being beamed up on *Star Trek*. Meanwhile, my brother, sister, and I stared into the pool as if mesmerized by the animals' antics, which in fact we soon were, given the hot sun beating down on our backs, the fox terrier's constant yapping, and the fact that our legs and feet soon fell asleep from kneeling.

"Stop squinting and don't scratch yourselves," Dad reminded us now and then as he shot roll after roll of film and moved the props and us around the pool.

After a while, Dad released us from our penitents' positions and had us pose individually. He photographed each of us with gerbils on our laps, climbing up our arms, sitting in our pockets, crawling across our shoulders, and staring at us nose to nose. I was so pleased to win Dad's praise for my ease in handling the gerbils that I nearly told him my secret right then. I wanted to introduce him to Kinky, safely in her cage in the garage. She would be a great gerbil model—and then we wouldn't have to sell her. But Dad was in such a fugue state of fevered concentration that conversation was impossible. Besides, he would have disapproved of me disobeying his orders.

Occasionally that afternoon, a gerbil would fall asleep on duty and we'd have to prod it with a finger or a stalk of grass to get it moving again in the wading pool. Toward the end of the session, a gerbil bit Donald's finger so hard that he began shaking his hand frantically to dislodge its little teeth, which of course only made the animal hang on to the finger with all of its mighty rodent power.

At this, I laughed until my sides hurt. Dad went pale and ordered my mother to "do something." Mom, who had grown up on a farm and knew how to bridle a horse, shear a sheep, and throttle a chicken, came to the rescue by pinching the gerbil's jaws open. There wasn't nearly as much blood as I'd hoped.

At last, as the sun was setting and streaks of pink were floating like forgotten scarves along the brackish water behind us, we were released. We ran to the pitcher of lemonade that Mom had put out on the screened porch. Our skin was slick with sweat and our legs were crisscrossed by grass tracks and dotted red from the chiggers. But that didn't matter, because Dad was pleased.

"You did a great job today, kids," he told us, and handed Donald and me a dollar apiece.

Donald and I were so busy plotting ways to spend our sudden good fortune that we forgot to ask Dad why he wanted so many pictures of us with gerbils.

~

IN THE middle of August, Dad shipped off to sea for another four months. We went to see him off at the pier. Mom looked Barbie-doll gorgeous in her white flowered sundress with its full skirt; she even had a red handbag to match her red high heels. Every man in uniform smiled at her, the beautiful dark-haired wife of their ship's commanding officer, as the sailors in their white uniforms poured like milk up the clanging gray metal ramp.

It was a typical Virginia summer day, the heat so strong that it cast puddle mirages on the docks. As we waited for the sailors and Marines to board the ship, Donald, Gail, and I pelted rocks at the jellyfish that flowered blue and purple in the water below the pier. The water was a deep frothy green, like liquid spinach, and we took turns pretending to push each other into the ocean.

Truthfully, the idea of falling into the water terrified me, for Dad's ship rose out of it like a monolith, and it was easy to imagine being sliced in half by its giant nose. The USS *Grant County* looked like an enormous car ferry, only instead of sedans and station wagons it carried tanks and giant trucks and Marines. From Dad's lectures at dinner, I knew that it was 446 feet long, was powered by six diesel engines, had a troop capacity of 706, traveled at speeds of seventeen knots, and had three gun mounts.

"It's one heck of a boat," Dad always said, "and I'm proud to be at her helm."

Donald and I occasionally played onboard the USS *Grant County* that summer, trying out the hideaway beds and metal bathroom sinks scarcely bigger than cereal bowls, and banging our shins on the high oval doorways when we played tag. We sneaked into the forbidden areas, too, like the cargo hold, where we'd hide behind vehicles as big and impossible-looking as dinosaurs, their treads still harboring flattened bamboo stalks from lands I couldn't imagine.

On this day, though, Mom wouldn't let us board the ship.

She told us the men were busy getting ready to go to the Mediterranean, "in case there's a little brush fire somewhere that needs putting out. Those Communists could be hiding anywhere, you know." The way she said it made me imagine Communists as careless campers who might be thoughtless enough to toss a lighted match into dry brush.

Dad kissed us all good-bye. As he leaned down in my direction, the brim of his hat hit my nose and we both laughed. Dad kissed my cheek then, and gave my arm a squeeze. "I know you'll be good for your mother," he said. "You always are. But I want you to do something for me, too."

I nodded, solemn and responsible despite Donald making faces at me from the edge of the dock. "I'll do what I can, Dad."

"Help your mom take care of the gerbils," he said. "She still doesn't like them much."

"No, Dad. But I do."

"That's my girl." He kissed me one more time, then turned to my mother and hugged her briefly before making his way up the gangplank without us, his uniform whiter than anyone's.

Chapter Three

Even Girls Like Gerbils!

Unlike my brother Donald

CREDIT: D. G. ROBINSON JR.

We had many modeling sessions with gerbils that first year in Virginia. The true purpose of my father's photography sessions was not revealed to us, however, until a box of books arrived one day while we were at school. Dad handed one of the books around the dinner table that night as Mom ladled creamed tuna with peas over the saltine crackers on our plates.

The book was called *How to Raise and Train Pet Gerbils* and had my dad's name on the cover. To my horror, Donald's picture was on the cover, too. The photograph showed my brother balancing a pair of gerbils in the crook of his arm. He was dressed in a bright blue shirt that set off his blond hair, and the camera added so many pounds that my pickleheaded brother looked nearly handsome.

The same portrait of Donald lovingly cradling those two gerbils appeared again inside the book, with this noble caption: "The author's son handles gerbils without fear by either party."

On the opposite page, I made my own solo debut in my red-striped blouse, with a gerbil on one shoulder and this humiliating proclamation beneath my picture: "Even girls like gerbils!"

"They paid me three hundred dollars for this book," Dad told us proudly.

"Good thing the models and props were free," Mom said.

Dad ignored this. He was busy explaining how his book was part of a popular series published by T.F.H. (Tropical Fish Hobbyist) Publications in New Jersey, a company owned by Herbert R. Axelrod. "That man is one of the world's last true eccentrics," Dad added.

"Not like anybody we know," Mom said.

"What does Mr. Axelrod do, Dad?" I asked.

"When he's not publishing books, Herb travels to the Amazon to catch new species of fish and names them all after himself," Dad said. "And when he's not doing that, he lives on Long Island in a huge mansion with a bomb shelter."

"I wouldn't mind a little mansion," Mom said, tapping the ashes of her cigarette onto her dinner plate. "Maybe you should write another book for him."

Dad had already thought of that. "Herb and I think I should write my next book about collared lizards," he announced, in a way that made Mom light another cigarette before she'd finished the first one. Meanwhile, Dad informed us that his gerbil book was already "selling like hotcakes," and we kids should always remember that in business, "the secret of success is timing, just like catching a wave at Virginia Beach."

When Mom snorted at this, Dad produced evidence. "The world was ready for my book," he insisted. "I hit it right with this one, Sally. Look at these." He produced a file of newspaper and magazine clippings from his briefcase. Dad often brought his briefcase to the dinner table with him, "just like an Amway salesman," Mom observed.

One of the articles, from the April 15, 1966, issue of *Time,* was called "Happiness Is a Pocket Kangaroo," and compared gerbils favorably to hamsters.

"Pets that are fun to play with, easy to care for and that thrive in captivity are hard to come by," I read aloud to Donald and Gail while my parents argued. "For the past decade, the furry favorite has been the hamster, but it tends to be neurotic, eat its young and bite the hand that feeds it. Now another member of the rodent family has arrived on the scene, warming children's hands and parents' hearts wherever its fuzzy face appears. It is the Mongolian gerbil (pronounced jurbill), a ball of fluff only four inches long (plus three inches of tufted tail) that looks and leaps like a vest-pocket kangaroo."

The article noted that gerbils were so popular by now that they had even appeared on the NBC children's program *Birthday House* and that singer Barbra Streisand had raved about her pair of gerbils on her CBS special.

In prowling through libraries, Dad had also unearthed a photo spread from the October 13, 1966, issue of the New York *Sunday News* called "New Look in Pets"; one picture in that series demonstrated a woman holding a gerbil "comfortably" in a wineglass.

"I'm telling you, Sally," Dad said, waving his Camel cigarette over his dinner plate. "Everyone is climbing onto the gerbil bandwagon. By the time I write about collared lizards, there's going to be a hot market for those, too."

My parents argued the pros and cons of raising lizards through dinner. Mom was against the idea; she'd been disappointed by too many reptiles in the past. She reminded Dad of Mr. Green Jeans, an iguana we'd named after Donald's favorite character on the TV show *Captain Kangaroo*. Mr. Green Jeans was so tame that he would ride on your shoulder even while you pretended your bicycle was a horse. Then Mom turned the heat lamp off in his aquarium to save on electricity bills, figuring the lizard would be warm enough because it was summer. Sadly, the air-conditioning froze Mr. Green Jeans to death right on his sleeping branch.

We'd also had a pair of horned toads with devil heads. The horned toads were speckled black and white, and you could hardly see them on the aquarium gravel. They weren't very friendly, either; they'd flatten themselves against the bottom of the aquarium if you tried to pick them up, opening their mouths like they wanted to swallow you whole even though they were only four inches long. The horned toads eventually starved to death because we didn't ever manage to feed them the right mealworms and they wouldn't eat anything else.

There was a lesson in this, Mom pointed out. "It doesn't pay to be picky if you live in a cage," she warned as she swept the horned toads with their gravel into the kitchen trash.

Now she told Dad that she had washed her hands of reptiles forever, and stood up to gather dishes. "Holly, come help me in the kitchen. Donald, if you give that dog one more green bean under the table, I'm going to feed you under the table with him. Get back into your chair."

I followed Mom out to the kitchen. "Do you really think Dad's right?" I asked, as I helped her rinse plates. "Is his gerbil book going to be a big hit?"

"Well, it's not like the Beatles," she said. "Nobody's going to faint at the sight of it."

~

My father's book probably never did make anyone faint, but it did have a long shelf life. Dad wasn't surprised. "It really is the definitive book on gerbils," he said with satisfaction.

It's true that the pages of *How to Raise and Train Pet Gerbils* were packed with pithy how-to advice on selecting, feeding, training, and even breeding pet gerbils. But what probably made the book a best seller was a combination of lucky timing, as Dad took care to remind us; his full-color photographs of gerbils at their most beguiling (my favorite showed a gerbil standing on its hind legs next to a miniature stuffed red kangaroo); and his writing, which was nothing like our father's conversational style.

At home, we were used to Dad's barked commands ("Sit up straight!" "Don't jump on the couch!" "Put your napkin on your lap!" "Be quiet so I can think!") and ongoing safety seminars ("Never drink out of your glass and walk at the same time"; "Never take a shower or talk on the telephone during a lightning storm"). In my father's world, accidents didn't just happen. They were caused by human error. His job was to make us conscientious and cautious, and thus prepared for life's big curveballs.

However, in *How to Raise and Train Pet Gerbils,* my father was generous and funny, acutely observant and understanding of the flaws of others. He also liked to spice up his writing with similes and exclamation marks. In the section about gerbil "locomotion," for instance, he wrote, "Young gerbils can use their hind legs for jumping by the time they're weaned. When a cage full of youngsters is suddenly startled, they look like a box of jumping beans scattering in various directions! The owner has owned some which seemed to enjoy doing back-flips!" During a jump, Dad added, the tail "may act like a rudder to help guide the animal through the air."

To my shock, Dad also seemed to know that I'd been handling the gerbils. Under "Selecting Pet Gerbils," he wrote, "Although the author's 10-year-old daughter has tamed 'middle-aged' gerbils in a few days, it is more desirable to begin training with a younger animal."

My father had never spoken to me about his suspicions, so I'd assumed he hadn't noticed that I was playing with the gerbils. After all, he didn't know how old I was—I was nearly twelve years old, not ten—and he didn't even know what class I was in at school, as we discovered when Dad drove to school to pick me up for a doctor's appointment and came back home again without me, furious because he thought I'd skipped school, since nobody had been able to locate me in the fourth grade. (I was in fifth.)

After reading that passage in Dad's book, I waited for him to confront me about playing with the gerbils. He never did. Still, I wondered if he'd written a particular passage under a section labeled "Escapes" just for me. Here, Dad described how to catch a renegade gerbil with a bucket:

> *Place a bucket in the room where your gerbil escaped. Make a series of "steps" from the floor up to the bucket lip, using wood blocks or bricks. Put some seeds and bedding on the steps and in the bucket; you can also put the escaped animal's mate inside the bucket (ensure that the bucket is high enough that the animals can't jump out). By the next*

morning your escaped gerbil should be safely in the bucket and ready for return to his cage.

~

BY THE time I started sixth grade, we had more than 250 gerbils in our Virginia garage. Dad had added extra shelves for them, and we could no longer park our car indoors. Mom simply waved a hand at nosy neighbors who asked why we always left the cars in the driveway. "Oh, I've never been much good at backing out," she'd say. "And it's so much easier to bring groceries in through the front door, don't you think?"

Dad went back to sea for four months. Donald was hardly around, either; he and his friends had built a fort out of forgotten cement pipes, creating a lid for it out of scrap wood. Lately they'd been busy designing homemade bombs; occasionally, riding my bike around the neighborhood, I'd hear an explosion and know Donald was at work.

Mom was busy, too. She still trolled the flea markets and had developed a new passion: clocks. We had more than our share of them, all ticking and chiming and bonging and cuckooing as they struggled to keep time. Mom was also such a devotee of the psychic healer Edgar Cayce that she made several trips to Cayce's house in Virginia Beach and schooled herself in extrasensory perception. We practiced ESP with her, guessing what was for lunch or where she'd hidden her hairbrush, and "seeing" the numbers she pictured in her mind. Mom even arranged for Edgar Cayce's son Hugh to lecture at one of her champagne brunches for the Navy wives.

My mother's ESP fortunately did not extend to the

garage, where Marcy and I were personally testing Dad's new marketing tool for schools and pet shops: a mimeographed handout called "20 Simple, Humane Experiments with Gerbils for Schools or Individuals." Throughout that fall, we did all twenty gerbil experiments and recorded the results in black laboratory notebooks that Marcy's mother bought for us at thc Navy commissary when we said we needed them for school.

One of our favorite experiments was #2, "The Senses." This involved mixing artificial sunflower seeds with real seeds. As my dad instructed in the purple ink of his mimeographed instructions, we meticulously recorded "the degree of success in selection of real food under conditions of normal light and in darkness."

Along with being an expert furniture maker, Dad had been carving fake sunflower seeds in his spare time. Marcy and I discovered the wooden seeds, perfect in every detail, cached in a matchbox on his workbench. We fed these decoys to the garaged gerbils, alternately flicking the lights on and off to see what they'd do. Most of the animals seemed happy enough to gnaw on them without actually swallowing; they trimmed those decoy seeds as sharp as pencil points.

We also tried experiment #3, "Locomotion." For this laboratory exercise, Dad advised amateur animal scientists to "measure approximate maximum speed of locomotion with an unconfined gerbil in an escape-proof room."

Marcy and I eagerly tried doing this with two gerbils, but we failed to measure the speed since the garage proved not to be escape-proof after all. While Marcy stood at the far end of the garage with a stopwatch at the finish line we'd marked in tape, I released our rodent sprinters near Dad's workshop table. To our dismay, the animals dashed right by Marcy, flattened themselves to envelope size, and easily passed beneath the garage door. By the time we raised the door to follow, the gerbils were tumbling like dried brown leaves across the paved road to a neighbor's neatly edged lawn. We never recovered our subjects.

After that, Marcy and I retreated to safer experiments, such as #12: "Gnawing Ability." This required nothing more challenging than giving various groups of gerbils pieces of wood to chew on, recording their gnawing rates, and describing the shapes they made. This was a fun experiment to record, because while most gerbils would chew up just about anything you gave them, a few seemed to understand that this was their chance to shine. One gerbil, in particular, had the soul of an artist, chewing a little and then sitting back on her hind legs to examine her work before going at it again. We went through an entire box of my sister's ABC building blocks before Mom found out.

Afterward, we did as my father suggested and made a display out of each "unique wood sculpture" by gluing them into shoeboxes that we'd painted, creating dioramas of gerbil art. Gail was as pleased as we were with the results, but Mom made me babysit around the neighborhood until I'd earned enough money to replace my sister's set of blocks.

~

SHORTLY after Dad returned from sea duty, Donald and I were watching *The Jetsons* on TV in the den. We were debating whether it would be cooler to have an ejecting bed that could pop you out like a toaster or a vacuum tube that could shoot you off to school when Dad burst into the house from the side door to the garage, flailing his arms as if he were being chased by hornets. His hairless head gleamed as pink and shiny as a dog's nose.

"One of the gerbils is having a seizure!" he yelled.

Mom, who was sitting on the couch with Gail, pulled my little sister closer, as if to prevent her from catching whatever lunatic fever had infected our father. "What do you mean, a seizure?" she asked.

"Damn it, I don't know!" Dad called over his shoulder as he jogged down the hallway toward his study. "The animal just started shivering and trembling and twitching its whiskers, and then it froze right up stiff!"

"Maybe it's dying," Mom suggested, just this side of hopeful.

"I don't think so," Dad said.

He returned a minute later, carrying his camera and hurrying back to the garage, still talking fast. "I picked the gerbil up by its tail, and it flopped around and seemed like it was filled with jelly. But then, a minute later, it started running around like nothing had happened."

We all raced into the garage after him to witness the miraculous seizing gerbil, which he'd confined to an empty plastic cage. Dad was right: the animal looked normal. But when he picked it up out of its cage and dropped it gently into another empty cage beside it, the gerbil flattened out and bared its teeth, trembling so violently that I tried to stroke its back to calm it.

Mom snatched me away by the wrist. "Don't you dare touch that animal," she said. "It looks rabid."

"It can't have rabies," Dad scoffed. "What rabid animal could get into the garage in the middle of the night and bite a gerbil?"

"A muskrat," she suggested. "A raccoon. A cat."

Dad shook his head. "And bite a gerbil through a plastic cage without eating it for a midnight snack? I doubt it. And it's not like any of the gerbils could get out of the garage on their own."

"Just the same, I'm going inside," Mom said. "You and the kids should, too. We should get rid of that gerbil before it infects somebody else."

She left the garage with Donald and Gail and closed the door firmly behind her, but I stayed behind with Dad. Guiltily, I thought of the gerbils that had escaped while Marcy and I were playing with them. Dad had never noticed them missing because he was at sea.

I thought about Kinky, too, whose life I had saved when Dad discovered the crook in her tail and called her "a defect." He wanted to "dispose of her" in the same mysterious way he did with other gerbils that didn't suit his purposes, an activity he did at night after we were in bed. I assumed that he drowned them in the lake, but he never admitted to this. I had pleaded with him for Kinky's life, though, and he let her live in a separate cage. I still took her out and brought her into the house to play with now and then. Could Kinky have somehow gotten rabies while she was out of the cage?

"Are you positive that gerbil doesn't have rabies?" I asked Dad. The gerbil appeared to have recovered completely, and sat up now on its hind legs to stare at us as we stared at it.

"Absolutely," he said. "This animal is simply subject to seizures, like an epileptic," he explained.

I knew all about epilepsy because Laura Troisi, a new girl in my sixth-grade classroom, had it. Each time Laura had a seizure, the teacher held her down by the legs while the nurse pressed a tongue depressor between Laura's foaming lips, shouting, "Don't let the poor thing swallow her tongue!"

Once, I'd even been the one chosen by the teacher to hold Laura's legs until the nurse arrived. I tried hard not to look at Laura's underpants as she flopped around on the cold tile floor, but I could see that she wore day-of-the-week underpants like mine. As noble as I felt for being the one chosen to hold the afflicted in place, it bugged me that Laura had worn Wednesday underpants on a Thursday. The feel of Laura's cool fishy skin made me shiver, too, and I had to be brave not to make a face at the nubby feel of the black leg hair stubble sprinkled on her skin like pepper.

"Maybe some gerbils can get epilepsy, but others can't," I suggested. "Like people."

"You're probably right, Holly," Dad said. "Or maybe all gerbils can have seizures, but it has to be the right combination of environmental factors to set them off. I don't really know."

Even though the gerbil in question appeared completely normal again, Dad kept it in a cage by itself after that, just in case there was something wrong with it. From then on, he spent every free minute in the garage, doing everything in his power to induce seizures in gerbils. When I asked why, he muttered, "This could be my big scientific breakthrough."

I liked the sound of that. What if my father wasn't just a

Navy commander with a secret stash of gerbils but a genius scientist, like Einstein or Madame Curie? And, by extension, if Dad was a genius, maybe there was hope for me, even if the art teacher at school had just called me a retard for painting my self-portrait blue.

Some nights I sat on the stepladder in the garage and watched my father at work until Mom sent me to bed. Dad was so intent on the gerbils that he never acknowledged my presence while engaging in various seizure-inducing tactics: shining lights into a gerbil's eyes, flicking the garage lights on and off, moving gerbils between cages, or holding them upside down by their tails before flipping them right side up again.

"About the only thing you haven't done is yell 'Boo!' in their faces," Mom observed one Saturday morning.

Afterward, we heard Dad shouting at the gerbils in the garage.

~

As Dad conducted his gerbil experiments with increasing intensity, he also began writing to veterinarians and researchers around the country, searching for someone else who might have made the same observations of this bizarre rodent behavior. Eventually he got lucky. Dr. Sigmund T. Rich, director of the research animal facility at the University of California, Los Angeles, wrote back to tell Dad that although he had never seen seizures among the gerbils in his lab, he'd sure like to.

"Film it for me," Dr. Rich suggested. "I want to see what you're talking about."

So Dad promptly hung up a white sheet in his office as a

backdrop and filmed an 8 mm movie of gerbils having seizures. "This is the first and only such movie in the world," he told us as he set off for the post office to mail the movie all the way to California.

"I'm sure it's unique," Mom said. "In a class all by itself."

I was finally old enough to understand that if Mom said things a certain way, she was really saying the opposite of what she thought, so you'd better listen closely. But despite her doubts about Dad's genius, Dr. Rich was so impressed by the movie that he encouraged Dad to write an article.

"But what would you say in an article?" I asked Dad, daring to stand in the doorway of his home office, a sanctuary so off-limits that you couldn't even borrow a pair of scissors without having to clean out the car as a punishment for crossing the forbidden threshold.

"I'd just describe what I've seen our gerbils do in the garage, I guess," Dad said. "There are lots of scientists who might be interested in that sort of behavior." He explained that he'd combed through all of the scientific papers he could find about gerbils in the library. "I've discovered something that could potentially change the way people do medicine, " Dad said, lifting his chin a little. "No other laboratory animal has natural seizures. For mice and rats and other lab animals, seizures have to be induced through electric shock, sound waves, or vitamin deficiencies. Gerbils are unique."

I wasn't surprised. I'd discovered for myself that gerbils were unique. Kinky knew her name and would take sunflower seeds from my lips. She could find her way through a maze of blocks to whatever bit of lettuce or carrot I'd put there for her.

She'd curl up on my shoulder while I read a book, too, and nibble gently at the tips of my hair when she was ready to climb down.

"That's great, Dad," I said. "Maybe you can write a book about gerbil seizures instead of collared lizards."

"I've already started another book," Dad said, "and it's got nothing to do with lizards."

That year, Dad self-published a second book, called *Raise Gerbils as Pets, Laboratory Animals*. In it, he spelled out his dreams for the future:

> *A part-time business is, and no doubt always will be, a part of the great "American Dream," especially if this part-time business can be started at home. . . . Obviously, no one can predict the future with any degree of accuracy, but it is a fact that gerbils are the newest pets and experimental animals with any amount of popularity or promise since the hamster made his mark in this country about a generation ago. The present and past performances of the gerbil in this regard seem to indicate that he is following in the hamster's footsteps.*

Even now, decades later, it's hard for me to shake that absurd image of a gerbil following in a hamster's footsteps. Yet, I recognize the real truth underlying my father's words: nobody can predict the future, but somewhere between ordering his first four pairs of gerbils and writing those lines, my dad bet our family's entire future on the gerbil.

Chapter Four

A Navy Man in Kansas

Dad as a young officer

CREDIT: THE HOLLY ROBINSON COLLECTION

In the spring of 1961, Dad came home from working on his ship one night and gathered us in the den for a family meeting. He instructed Donald and me to sit on either side of the fireplace in our handcrafted pine thrones, while Gail colored at the giant cable spool that Dad had so cleverly turned into a coffee table.

By the envelope that Dad held between his hands, we knew he'd gotten his orders. For military families like ours, this was like Oscars night, since you never knew what that envelope contained. We all tried to sit still and be quiet as Dad began his usual speech about his duty to this great country and ours, too.

However, none of us was fully prepared for what the envelope contained. "When summer comes, this family is shipping off to Fort Leavenworth, Kansas," Dad announced.

"Kansas?" Mom repeated, like he'd said "Mars." "What the hell is the Navy doing in Kansas?"

"Teaching the Army about the Navy," Dad said.

Dad sounded matter-of-fact about this, but I could tell by

the pinched look around his blue eyes and the way he crumpled up the envelope and tossed it into the fireplace that he wasn't happy about this new tour of duty. Nonetheless, he explained that the Navy was asking him to teach Army officers what the Navy could do for them during wartime at the Command and General Staff College in Fort Leavenworth. "Given the events in Vietnam, Army officers have to be prepared to fight in wide-ranging circumstances," he told us, "from counterinsurgency attacks to full scale nuclear war. My job is to help teach them how."

So, in a peculiar sort of military Noah's ark, Dad was chosen as one of just three Navy officers assigned to Fort Leavenworth in 1967, along with three Marines and three Air Force officers. He had already served in the Korean War and visited ports and cities in more than thirty countries around the world. Now Dad sold our house in Virginia Beach and drove us to Kansas.

It was a miserable trip. By the time we left, it was July and so hot that our legs burned on the car seats even through the towels Mom gave us to sit on. Our white Ford Galaxy had no air-conditioning, so we were forced to ride with the windows down. We couldn't hear much or even keep our eyes open because of the wind and exhaust on the highway. Our parents chain-smoked throughout the drive, which meant that the smoke streamed steadily into the backseat.

At twelve years old, I suffered from such severe motion sickness that I was fed a steady diet of Dramamine. The drug turned me into a drooling narcoleptic. I woke up each time Donald pinched my leg, punched my arm, or ripped the book out of my hands, only to nod off again, my chin bouncing against my chest, until the blows accumulated and made me cry.

Once Mom turned around to snap at me in the car. "What in the world are you crying about?" she asked. "I can't understand why you're always so emotional, Holly. There's no need for this fuss. You know what it's like to move. Crying only makes things worse for all of us." She turned back around and said something I couldn't hear to my father.

It was true that I could remember what it was like to move. I had clear memories of all the places we'd lived, starting with our terraced gardens in Mexico City, where Dad was the naval attaché at the American embassy and did something mysterious with maps and Mom was a smash hit at parties in sparkling cocktail gowns that made her look like a mermaid. After that, there'd been a little red-shingled house and another, more solid brick house and several places in between. It didn't matter where I was, because I was at home with my family.

But I was older now, and it wasn't the house that I'd miss but the people and animals that had been woven into the fabric of my life in Virginia Beach. Marcy had become a second sister to me, and I was leaving her behind. My grandparents were staying in their apartment in Newport News. I didn't have my guinea pig, George, for comfort because my parents hadn't let me bring him; George was now living in a cage next to Marcy's rabbit. My parents had sold Tip and left Yankee, our newly adopted collie/shepherd, with our grandparents. The gerbils were all sold to pet stores or given away to schools, even Kinky, before Dad hosed out the garage and watered his little trees one last time. My whole world had been pulled out from beneath me like a scatter rug.

"Baby baby baby," Donald sang in my ear, pinching me as hard as he could, leaving red welts on my bare legs as the Summer of Love brought three hundred thousand protestors against the Vietnam War to New York.

Our family was in no mood for love-ins. Mom turned off the car radio and shook her head over the news of antiwar demonstrations not just in New York, where you'd expect that sort of thing, but all over the country, too. "Those dirty hippies," she said. "What do they know about duty?"

"They'll never last," Dad agreed.

Our only stop before Kansas was my father's childhood home in Ohio, where Donald and I slept in the stifling, slope-roofed attic room that had once belonged to Dad and his younger brother, Pete. The room was still full of fascinating relics: arrowheads and stamp collections, books on insects and BB guns, and the detritus of a boyhood spent dreaming of a world where every question has an answer.

~

THE oldest of three children, my father was born to Donald and Rebecca Robinson on April 21, 1928, in Montgomery, Ohio, a place that Dad always said had more churches than stores "because there's nothing to do there but plant your crops and pray."

According to my grandmother Robinson's diary, which I read many years after she died, "little Don-Don too often cuts up high jinks." By age two, my dad had reached the point where he "jabbers all day, says 'no' to everything," and "is always asking 'What's that?'" He "pulled the butterfly table over on him" one day, "burned his fingers on the oil stove" the next, and managed to pry the cover off an electrical outlet, earning an electric shock for his curiosity.

While noting that "Don-Don has learned to spit—also lots of other things," Grandmother Robinson revealed her survival strategy, which turned out to be the same one I use now with my youngest son Aidan: "I try to keep Don-Don outside as much as I can."

What sort of twisted path would lead such a child into gerbil farming instead of into other, possibly more logical career options, such as dynamiting bridges?

Here's where the nurture part of the nature-versus-nurture debate comes in: children absorb every experience that comes their way, but only some stick. You can't tell until years later which childhood experiences will become permanent features of their interior landscapes as adults.

In my dad's case, he experienced early on that raising animals at home could be profitable. One of his childhood neighbors in Ohio, Frank Maxfield, was a chemist employed by Procter and Gamble who raised mice, rats, hamsters, rabbits, and guinea pigs in a blue barn behind his peak-roofed farmhouse. Maxfield sold the animals to research scientists at various institutions. My father played with Maxfield's children and envied their extra spending money. He longed to live more like they did. Or, even better, like the Fleischmann family, whose palatial Yeast Estate was just down the road.

Dad's own family lived in a modest white box of a house next to the railroad tracks. Once a week, the steam engine ran behind the Robinson home from Montgomery to Blue Ash, making it a natural stop for ragmen and train tramps who begged for food at the kitchen door. Before World War II, Dad's father ran a gas station, where he was once stabbed with an ice pick and another time kidnapped and taken out to a field, where the robbers poured whiskey down his throat and took his money.

Once the war started, Grandfather Robinson worked on an assembly line at the Wright Aircraft Factory. As a boy, my dad used to lie in bed at night and listen to the steady *zoom-zoom* sound of aircraft engines being tested, a sound that steadily fed his fantasies about joining the military.

By the time Dad hit high school, he was earning his own way by delivering newspapers and working in the local drugstore. The pharmacist trained my father to compound prescriptions, and by age sixteen Dad could fill them on his own. He used down time between customers to mix up his own gunpowder, wrap it in aluminum foil, and lay these delicious little dynamite capsules under the streetcar tracks at regular intervals, so that it sounded like a machine gun firing when the trolley went by.

Dad had his own pets—he was especially fond of white mice—but he longed to be a world-famous explorer like Martin Johnson and bring back new species "from darkest Africa." Johnson, who left home at fourteen to work on a cattle boat, later became the first filmmaker to capture classic aerial scenes of giraffes and elephants stampeding across the African plains. My father watched Johnson's movies by sneaking into the local drive-in movie theater on foot, but the closest he came to being Martin Johnson was a mail-order taxidermy course he took in high school that cost him $12 of his hard-earned drugstore money. Completing his taxidermy assignments required walking up and down the rural roads of Ohio to find dead birds and animals. Dad enthusiastically ordered the accessories he needed to complete his projects—squirrel skulls and birds' eyes—through catalogs, just as he would order his first gerbils more than twenty years later.

My father's thorough understanding of animal physiology and anatomy would come in handy, like when he was making his own mini-documentaries of gerbils suffering seizures in our Virginia garage. First, though, Dad had to escape the confines of Montgomery, Ohio.

Love led him to join the Navy. Dad's high school sweetheart was a fair-skinned, blue-eyed beauty named Ann Lloyd, whom he called "Angel Eyes." Ann and her family represented everything my dad longed to achieve. Ann's father, John T. Lloyd, owned Lloyd Pharmaceutical Company, which had made it big with Chigger-Ease. Her grandfather, John Uri Lloyd, was not only a research chemist but also a best-selling novelist. The family owned a vacation home with an inground pool—a rarity in Ohio back then—and a horse stable.

Before their high school graduation, a friend suggested that my father go to West Point. Dad took this idea to heart: West Point offered horsemanship classes, and Dad was bent on convincing Ann that he was worthy of her. He knew horses were the way to her heart. At the time, however, West Point had no vacancies, so my father's congressman nominated him to the Naval Academy instead.

Dad was admitted to Annapolis despite the fact that he couldn't swim and had never even seen the ocean. The Navy wasn't in my father's plans, but it was his ticket to adventure. He eagerly left Ohio and set forth to serve his country.

In return for his service, the Navy led him straight back to love. My mother's older brother, Donald Keach, joined the Navy and met my father during the Korean War, when both were young officers on the USS *John R. Pierce*. When my uncle Don was injured by gunfire on the *Pierce,* it was my father who was sent to accompany him home to Maine, where Dad met my mother.

"It was love at first sight," Dad still says, "just because of the way your mother looked up at me and laughed with those brown eyes."

At the time, Mom was a senior at the University of Maine and dating several different men. "Those were the days when every girl had just one goal, and that was to get married," she explained to me once. "Marriage was our very reason for being."

Men in the military had a certain aura, she said, and Dad had seen enough of the world to seem confident and decisive. He also had a movie star's height and lean physique, a strong jaw, blue eyes, and tight curls of sandy hair. To add to his appeal, after their first date, Dad went back to sea and wrote my mother "a drawerful of beautiful letters." She had graduated from the university by then and was working for a Maine newspaper while deciding between job possibilities at the UN, Pan Am, and the BBC in London.

"If you want to see the world, I'll show you the world," Dad promised during his next shore duty—officially, their third date—and confessed that he'd been thinking of asking her to marry him.

"Well, are you going to ask or aren't you?" my mother wanted to know.

Dad, forever the prepared Boy Scout, immediately pulled a little blue velvet bag out of his pocket and showed her the diamond inside it. "How do you want it set?" he asked.

"When I told him I wanted platinum, he gasped a little, but that's what I got," Mom told me. "Don't ever be afraid to ask for what you want in life."

Chapter Five

Doin' Time in Leavenworth

Our gerbil circus

CREDIT: E. G. ROBINSON JR.

Kansas looked nothing like the flat, dry, tornado- and witch-plagued land I knew from *The Wizard of Oz*. This Kansas was green and hilly and much prettier than the swampy Tidewater region of Virginia that was rapidly dimming in my memory as we drove mile after mile away from it. We'd been in the car forever, and so we were excited to arrive, especially when Dad explained that there were Indians living nearby. Donald imagined being scalped while I daydreamed about owning a silver horse like the Lone Ranger and having a best Indian friend of my own, one who rode a pinto pony bareback and warned me of dangers on the road ahead.

Mom, though, was not happy. She wasn't accustomed to spending so much uninterrupted time with Dad. Whenever they fought about something—usually his driving—she'd threaten to get on the next Greyhound bus traveling in the opposite direction. Being from Maine, she also viewed the Midwest as provincial and said she couldn't imagine living here, especially stuck on a fort surrounded by Army families.

"But what's the difference between the Army and the

Navy?" I asked. "I mean, other than working on land instead of on a ship?"

"Navy people are higher-class than Army," Mom explained. "In the Army, they just want bodies. You don't have to be smart to join."

To make matters worse, our fort housing wasn't vacant yet. We were relegated to living for a month in cramped enlisted men's quarters with no air-conditioning, thin walls, and a mysterious metal vent between the apartments big enough to pass a baby through. That first still, sticky night in Kansas, the noises seeping through the vent made it clear that the Army wife next door was no happier than my mother was to be cast away at Fort Leavenworth.

"You want out of here?" a man demanded.

"You know I do!" his wife screamed.

"Fine. I'll be first in line to buy you a plane ticket!"

Our parents fought that first night in Kansas, too, as Mom walked around the table serving mashed potatoes.

"So tell me," she said to my father. "What was the big goddamn rush to get here?" She dropped potatoes onto Gail's plate first, *slap*.

"Sally, watch your language," Dad said, giving each of us the hairy eye so that we'd know not to follow Mom's example.

"You could have gone ahead of me just this once to set up house," Mom said. She served the potatoes to Donald and me, *slap slap*. "The kids and I could have stayed with my mother."

"Your mother." Dad rolled his eyes. "Your mother, the Queen Mary."

No sooner were these words out than Mom slapped the

scoop of mashed potato smack onto my father's bald head instead of onto his plate.

"Jesus Christ, Sally!" Dad yelled, swiping at his head with a napkin.

"Jesus Christ, Sally!" Gail crowed, spooning mashed potatoes from her plate onto her own head.

Donald went to the vent leading to the apartment next door and put his mouth close to the grille. "Hey, guys!" he shouted to the neighbors. "Did you hear that through the vent?"

~

THE Army finally housed us in a stately, high-ceilinged apartment on the first floor of a brick building dating back to the early 1900s, a prime spot on Fort Leavenworth's parade ground, a vast expanse of rolling lawn that served as our front yard and the training ground for lines of soldiers marching and shouting in the shimmering heat as they readied themselves for Vietnam.

That first year in Kansas, Donald frequented the rifle range, where he earned the rank of sharpshooter at age ten. He also enjoyed using the parade ground as a launching pad for the Estes rockets he ordered from a catalog. The rocket kits came with ample warnings about careful parental supervision, but since our parents were always busy, Donald set them off on his own. It didn't matter. With all of the practice gunfire around us, anyone who heard the blasts just assumed it was another military exercise. Meanwhile, I discovered that Fort Leavenworth was like a small city. I could go anywhere by foot or bicycle: stores, movies, the pool at the officers' club, and, most wondrous of all, the Fort Leavenworth Hunt Club, where I watched my favorite horses and riders with the ferocious devotion of a fanatic fan stalking rock stars.

One night, I'd just rigged up an ingenious basket on a pulley and ropes that my friend John and I could use to deliver messages back and forth from his bedroom window upstairs to mine down below when I heard Dad come in. I went to my bedroom door, intending to close it, and saw my father scurrying in a peculiarly hunched way toward his own bedroom, hiding something under his coat.

I tugged on the rope, sent a message up to John saying I'd be back later, and ran down the hall. I found my mother in the kitchen, coloring with Gail. "Mom, he's doing it again," I hissed.

"Who?" she said without looking up.

"Dad! He's sneaking gerbils into the house under his coat!"

Mom took her time selecting a blue crayon and then lit a cigarette. She still wouldn't look at me. "Don't talk to me about it," she said. "Talk to your father."

"I will," I said. "I'll talk to him right now."

I went down the hall to their bedroom and knocked hard on the door. Dad didn't answer. I knocked again, harder.

The door opened a crack. "What is it?" Dad asked. "I'm busy."

Behind him, lights were set up on stands and shining against a white screen as a backdrop. I knew he'd bought three pairs of gerbils in a Kansas City pet shop shortly after our arrival; he kept them in our basement storage room, a dark and musty space, under lock and key. For the past week, Dad had been coming home after a full day of teaching and, as soon as the sun went down, he'd retreat to the basement and sneak back upstairs with gerbils stashed in his pocket or a cage tucked under his jacket.

"I want to know what you're doing in there, Dad," I said.

"What do you mean, what am I doing?" He didn't open the door any wider. With the bright lights behind him, my father's thin face was cast in shadow, his blue eyes dark pools. "I'm working," he said. "What did you think I'd be doing? I'm always working."

"I want to know why you have to sneak the gerbils up and down the stairs," I said. "Can't you just photograph them on the lawn like you did in Virginia?"

Dad looked at me like he was the one in his right mind. "Are you kidding me?" he asked. "Look, you can't tell anyone, not *anyone,* about the gerbils in the basement," he said. "Not even the other two Navy families at Fort Leavenworth. I could be discharged if the higher-ups found out what I'm doing. Now go on. I have to finish something here." He closed the door.

I didn't have to ask who the higher-ups were because I knew: the mysterious military brass, the generals and admirals housed in the Pentagon, a building that Dad told us was so vast, you had to wear roller skates to make it to appointments on time.

In the kitchen, my mother and sister were still coloring. "Mom," I said, "did you know that Dad's bringing his gerbils into your bedroom?"

"Yes, I know, honey."

"Don't you even care?" I demanded. "It's so strange! Can't you stop him?"

"Why should I?" Mom asked. She stood up and went to the counter, which she began wiping again, though it was already clean. "That's your father's thing. I don't have to know every last detail of what my husband does with his spare time. You won't, either, if you're smart."

She wrung out the dish rag, folded it in half, and laid it carefully over the kitchen faucet before finally turning around to look at me. "Look, I know it's bizarre, Holly, but that's your father."

~

WHAT was my father doing with a crop of gerbils in that dark, musty basement storage room?

He was breeding them again. The gerbils multiplied as easily in the basement as they had in our Virginia garage. We had a ten-by-twelve-foot space divided from the rest of the basement by thin walls—every apartment had a storage area like this—and Dad set up shelves for his gerbils just as he had in Virginia. Soon he had to move suitcases and odd boxes upstairs to make room for more shelves and gerbil cages. He continued to observe the gerbils and photograph them, so absorbed in his work that he made notes on a yellow pad of paper during dinner or held his head in his hands and gazed into space, his blue eyes unfocused. He might as well have been in a coma. Our family carried on dinner, conversations, arguments, and homework around him, as if Dad were a statue of himself.

While Dad trained Army officers at the Staff College to lead troops into Vietnam, he wrote a paper about gerbil seizures and the potential use of gerbils in research. The paper was accepted and published on January 6, 1968, in the prestigious journal *Science News* under the title "Animals Suited to Epileptic Research."

The first we heard about Dad publishing the results of his scientific studies was when he passed the magazine around the dinner table. He made sure to hold the magazine pages open with his own hands because he didn't want sticky pages, he said. In the article, he detailed his observations about gerbil seizures.

"After being handled," he'd written,

> *a susceptible animal may lie passively with limbs extended and body trembling, then resume normal activity within minutes. . . . Muscular rigidity sometimes molds the gerbil's body in specific postures or allows the animal to be held in positions it would not normally tolerate.*
>
> *More recently, moderate to severe seizures have been observed in some gerbils. This behavior is characterized by a staring appearance of the eye, falling down on the table, running movements of the legs, and a recovery period during which the gerbil appears dazed. Recovery is rapid and apparently complete; no deaths or aftereffects have been reported.*

Whatever my father couldn't capture in words about gerbil seizures, his photographs did it for him. Stark in black and white, one of the pictures showed a gerbil in full seizure. It looked like a monster in a low-budget Japanese horror movie. The gerbil's body was stretched out and stiff, and its tail stuck straight out. Its teeth were bared in a terrified grimace.

Proud as he was about having his first article appear in such an esteemed publication as *Science News,* my father never told anyone else at Fort Leavenworth about it. Nor did he indicate anywhere in the pages of the magazine that he was a Navy commander. In fact, he didn't even use his full name in the byline, only "D. G. Robinson Jr."

This magazine article brought correspondence from all over the world. I saw envelopes with university and laboratory names on the return addresses from as far away as Sweden and Japan. Apparently Dad wasn't the only man in the world with a thing for gerbils.

Encouraged by this brush with fame, he wrote a second piece for *Science News.* This one was published in the February 15, 1969, issue, and focused, surprisingly, not on gerbils but on sand rats and spiny mice.

Why would my father suddenly detour away from writing about the gerbil, the one thing that had succeeded in stirring up his passions to the point of forgetting all other outside pursuits?

Reading the article closely, I saw that the piece focused on diabetes and how the disease didn't occur naturally in sand rats, as it did in some mutant mice and certain strains of Chinese hamsters. To induce diabetes in sand rats, Dad reported, you had to feed them standard laboratory pellets. And in writing about spiny mice—also known as "porcupine mice"—in this piece, Dad listed research studies that revealed how spiny mouse females that had already given birth often acted as midwives to pregnant spiny mice if the mice were caged together.

The final paragraph of that paper is the only clue to Dad's surprising defection from gerbils. There, Dad wrote, "The availability of sand rats and spiny mice suggests that they will be valuable for studying many interrelated factors involved in diabetes . . . researchers hope to be able to establish stable inbred strains of these species to increase their potential as experimental animals."

In Kansas, Dad wasn't content to just sneak gerbils upstairs like James Bond with his latest secret weapon. He was toying with the idea that he might escape the military by retiring early and raising gerbils on a large scale while still keeping his options open by researching the potential of breeding other laboratory animals.

As always, though, he kept his plans a secret. My father's byline for the article on spiny mice and sand rats was again, simply, "D. G. Robinson Jr." Clearly, very few people reading *Science News* knew that the author of these papers was a Navy commander who went to work every day with gold bars on his shoulders, his lectures on naval war tactics timed to the Army minute.

And even fewer people at Fort Leavenworth knew what my dad was up to in the basement of our Army issue housing. Not even, most of the time, us.

Chapter Six

Trading My Bikini for a Horse

Ladybug

CREDIT THE HOLLY ROBINSON COLLECTION

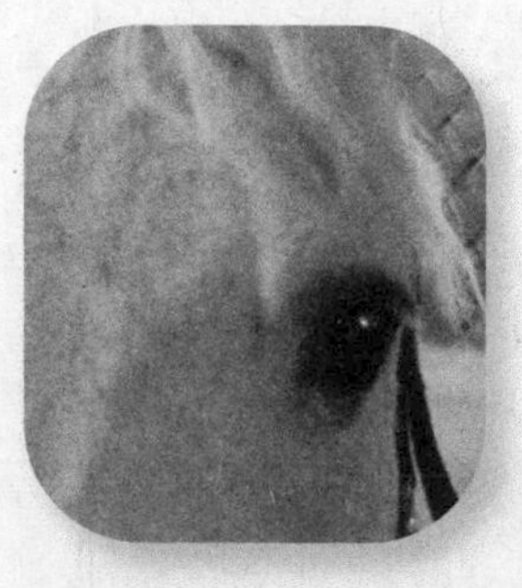

We arrived in Kansas the summer before I turned thirteen, and that time in my life was notable for this stunning achievement: my breasts and my bikini got me a horse.

"You've certainly started blossoming," Dad observed one day, looking up from the kitchen table to find me standing there in the new, two-piece green-and-white polka-dot bathing suit that I insisted on wearing everywhere, even biking past the lines of sweating uniformed soldiers to buy chewing gum and a Coke at the PX.

"Put something on, for God's sake," Mom said. When I refused and stomped out of the room, I heard her scolding my father. "We should never be living on an Army fort with a girl this age," she said. "Holly was such a sweet little thing when we brought her here, but now she's running wild."

She was right. Within two weeks of arriving in Kansas I'd found a crush, a blond, cleft-chinned colonel's son with his own basement band. He played lead guitar, wooing me with Iron Butterfly's "In-a-gadda-da-vita," and wore bangs dangerously close to his eyes.

When I wasn't with him, I roamed the fort with my new

best friend, Katy, the younger sister of one of the lifeguards at the officers' club pool. Our favorite pastime was to put on our bathing suits and follow the young soldiers around the base, teasing them with made-up marching songs of our own: "Left! Left! Left-right-left! I left my wife and forty-nine kids on the brink of starvation without any gingerbread!"

We also liked to hang out at the Hunt Club, flirting with the prisoners on work parole. Leavenworth is known for its prisons—the U.S. Penitentiary is there, as are Lansing Correctional Facility and the U.S. Military Disciplinary Barracks; the population is so prison-heavy that the Leavenworth Tourism Bureau adopted "Doin' Time in Leavenworth" as its marketing slogan one year. At the Hunt Club, the military prisoners mucked out stalls, mowed the hayfields, fed and watered the horses, worked out with weights in the tack room, and might as well have had *Danger!* tattooed on their chests, along with the usual assortment of skulls and eagles and women's names.

I was blossoming, but was I beautiful? I knew better. Yet I began wearing makeup and shaving what little hair I had on my legs. In an act of bravado that left me itching and thrashing about in my bed for weeks afterward, I even shaved off the hair on my back after Katy pointed it out.

"Mom," I asked in desperation one day, "do you think I'll ever be pretty?"

Her answer was less than encouraging. "We're so glad you're smart," she said. "And you'll be a wonderful mother."

In desperation, I took my looks for a test run. "Tell your brother I have a crush on him," I told Katy.

We had been lying next to each other at the pool, turning every ten minutes for an even tan, though my face was doomed to be pale because I always held a book up and read while sunbathing. Now I put the book down and watched as Katy, a big-boned blonde whose bathing suit never quite covered her fleshy behind, sauntered over to her equally big-boned blond brother and told him of my true and undying feelings.

Her brother squinted down at me from his lifeguard stand like Zeus observing the silly games of humans from Mount Olympus. Then he said something to his sister and turned away to blow his whistle at a boy jumping off the side of the pool. Katy trotted back, grinning, and flopped down on the towel beside me.

"He says you're not much in the face," she dutifully reported. "But you've got a great body. He said that he'd meet you after school if you want to learn how to French-kiss."

Later on, my face still burning from this assessment, I climbed onto a chair in the middle of my bedroom and started hissing cuss words. "Shit, bitch, fuck, crap, cunt!" I whispered viciously at the ceiling. "Damn, puke, crap, bastard!"

I ignored Donald, who sniggered just outside the door, until Mom came and pushed the door wide open.

"There," she said. "This way we can all hear you better. You must have something pretty important to say if you're standing up on a chair."

~

My only passion, other than my new bikini, was horses. I'd wanted one ever since I was a child, when I'd seen my mother climb onto the back of her Thoroughbred in Maine and ride off with a queen's distracted wave. For years I'd been reading every horse book I could find and living a rich fantasy life filled with mounts of every description. I had pretended that my pink and white bicycle was the Black Stallion as I raced the streets of Virginia, and I paced our hallways in Kansas as if I were leading my headstrong mustang pony, causing my parents to threaten to send me to charm school if I couldn't learn to "glide, not bounce," as Mom implored.

The Fort Leavenworth Hunt Club was paradise. The tack room to me was like the opium den to Sherlock Holmes. There were saddles and bridles and saddle blankets exuding those intoxicating odors of horse sweat and saddle soap. The wooden boxes were filled with brushes and crops and curry-combs and hoof picks. Men and women strode about purposefully in canary-yellow jodhpurs and black knee-high leather boots. And, of course, there were the horses, snorting and whinnying and running in the paddocks or munching hay in their stalls, their heads bobbing over stall doors, ears pricking as I whispered secrets to them or fed them carrots and apple slices out of my pockets.

I became a barn rat, helping other riders turn their horses out in the paddocks, where they rolled about in the dust, or volunteering to groom. I especially liked currying the horses' coats in slow circles, making the animals arch their necks in pleasure like big dogs being scratched behind the ears. I loved using the shedding blade, too: this was a long silver blade with sharp teeth and leather handles at either end that you pulled along the horses' bellies and flanks to make the loose hair rise in feathery wisps on the breeze.

If I didn't have a horse to work with, I'd just follow the older girls around, watching them closely as they flirted with the prisoners on work parole. The girls stood with one hand on a jodhpur-clad hip or tucked their hair beneath their velvet hunt caps as they smiled up at the angry, rebellious, muscle-bound men who did the cleaning and carpentry around the stables. I saw the power in these girls, power that came from their horses and the confident way they tamed these huge beasts with a cluck of the tongue and a bit of leather and leg.

I wanted to be them. I wanted to be like my mother. And, like the girl detective Trixie Belden, one of my favorite fictional heroines because she survived rabid dogs and poisonous snakes while solving dark mysteries, I longed for a horse of my very own. At times I even went around quoting the opening dialogue from *The Secret Mansion,* with the appropriate dramatic gestures.

"Oh, Moms," I'd moan, running my fingers through my short, sandy curls. "I'll just *die* if I don't have a horse."

"Why are you calling me that?" Mom would respond. "Stop whining. If wishes were horses, you'd have stables full of them by now."

Finally, though, she gave in. As Mom reasoned with my father, sitting on a horse under the watchful eye of an Army instructor had to be safer for me than spending free hours in some teenager's smoky basement or taking my new breasts for a strut around the pool. She convinced him to buy a small gray mare that I named Ladybug because Trixie Belden's first mount was called Lady.

People came and went from Fort Leavenworth every few months or years as Army orders dictated, and they rarely took their horses with them. The lieutenant colonel who sold us

Ladybug just days before he was sent to Vietnam assured us that the mare was "child-safe."

Ladybug certainly looked docile enough, with her long-lashed doe's eyes, sweet brown freckles, round belly, and snow-white mane and tail. However, my new mount had a nasty habit of holding her breath whenever she was saddled, so it was impossible to get the girth tight. Later, we'd learn the knack of fastening the girth and then giving the mare a sharp knee jab to the belly to get her to expel her breath while we cinched the saddle tighter. But that first day, Mom mounted Ladybug, urged her to trot around the ring, and immediately found herself hanging upside down and being dragged through the dust by one stirrup.

"That horse is cute but tricky," Mom pronounced when she managed to get herself untangled and dusted off.

Dad eyed my new horse with suspicion. "That animal doesn't seem child-safe to me," he said. "What if Holly gets hurt?"

"Oh, she'll be fine," Mom said breezily, trying not to limp as she led Ladybug over to the mounting block. "You have to get thrown at least thirty times before you're a real rider." My mother pulled herself back into the saddle, wincing just a little. This time the horse behaved, trotting and cantering smartly about the ring, tossing her head just like all of my fantasy horses had tossed theirs.

"Maybe we should try to get our money back," Dad said when Mom finished riding and handed the reins to me.

"Don't be ridiculous. I'm sure the owner's already parachuted into some Vietnamese jungle," Mom said.

I took Ladybug's reins and quickly led her out of earshot of my parents. "You're the most beautiful horse in the whole world," I whispered, stroking her velvety gray muzzle. "I'm going to wear a picture of you in my locket."

Ladybug was the sort of horse "who feels her oats," as my instructor put it, bucking and spooking sideways whenever the wind whipped up mini-tornadoes in the dusty riding ring, or trying to rub me off on a tree the minute my seat was loose. Within six months, though, I was a competent enough rider to start entering equitation classes in the local horse shows, and Ladybug and I won ribbons and trophies together.

My true love was trail riding, though, which brought a measure of peace not only to me but also to my mother, who would get babysitters for Gail and ride with me on a horse she'd bought for herself, an elegant bay Thoroughbred named Robin. When we were out on the bridle trails, alone on the narrow paths that wound through the fields and woods of Fort Leavenworth, it was as if she and I had assumed false identities and traveled to a foreign country.

With nothing more to disturb us than birdsong and the soft snorting sounds of the horses, we were transported far away, and never fought the way we did at home. On the trails, on our horses, my mother and I were almost friends.

Chapter Seven

Dad Buys Himself a Gerbil Farm

From GERBILS IN THE CLASSROOM

CREDIT: D. G. ROBINSON JR. AND VICTOR SCHWENTKER

When the gerbils first arrived at our Virginia ranch house, they were accompanied by a thin pamphlet on the history and care of gerbils written by Victor Schwentker. Victor lived in Brant Lake, New York, a hamlet in the Adirondack Mountains just west of Lake Champlain, a place where only the hardiest tourists make their way to cool off in the summer or enjoy a few glorious days of kaleidoscopic leaf peeping in the fall. It's an unlikely place for gerbils to make their first appearance in this country, but that's where their U.S. story began. It was only natural that my father, in his pilgrimage to know the gerbil, eventually wanted to tap in to Schwentker's expertise.

During our last year in Kansas, Dad and Victor began corresponding. Dad wrote his letters on the manual typewriter in his home office, and we'd hear the steady *tap-tap-tap* of the keys as the rest of us watched television in the next room, the sound of Dad's fingers on his typewriter as methodical and relentless as rain on a metal roof.

Dad read Victor's letters aloud to our mother sometimes, after Gail was in bed and Donald and I were settled in front of the television. He'd underline pertinent passages in the red pencil he used for marking papers at the Staff College, keeping it poised to highlight key passages as he and Mom discussed the content of the letters. I paid little attention to these ramblings and caught only bits and pieces of the conversations.

Still, I understood that Victor Schwentker was my father's idol. Victor was the sort of man who'd see a road and want to know where it went. As a young man, he had traveled down to South America to break polo ponies and then back up to Canada to run moonshine. Eventually he tried to settle down and worked as an engineer for General Electric in Philadelphia, where he met and married his wife, Mildred West, a society girl teaching private school. When the Depression cost Victor his job, the pair retreated to Brant Lake, where they lived at West Farm, Mildred's childhood summer home.

At first, the Schwentkers eked out a living by renting out summer cottages and selling milk and butter from their cows and vegetables from their gardens to the summer people. They had one child, a daughter, and Mildred, who was forty years old by the time she became a mother, longed to return to Philadelphia. But Victor was thriving on the farm. He'd finally landed in the one place that felt like home. Now he just had to find a way to stay there.

It was Victor's brother, Francis Schwentker, M.D., a Navy officer and well-known pediatric researcher, who gave him the means: Francis talked Victor into raising laboratory animals on the farm instead of cows. Francis was working with the military to develop vaccines for tropical diseases, and he knew there was a shortage of quality laboratory animals for scientific studies.

Victor renamed their homestead Tumblebrook Farm and

began with a colony of rabbits. Most of his business came from the military, which was shipping thousands of U.S. soldiers to the Pacific to fight in World War II. Military strategists had recognized during World War II that their deadliest enemies weren't the opposing forces, but the infectious diseases the U.S. troops would encounter for the first time abroad. Developing the necessary vaccines and treatments for these new pathogens was a formidable challenge and would require many animals for experimentation. Thanks to this new military push for medical miracles and his handy family connection, Victor was soon providing not only rabbits but also guinea pigs and mice to researchers around the country. For many years, Tumblebrook Farm was like a Navy installation, complete with guards posted to keep the animals safe from evil Axis powers. Employees who worked there were even exempt from the draft, because what they were doing was considered so important.

Like my own father, Victor designed and hand-crafted anything he could, whether it was a new kind of cage or a milking machine for guinea pigs. Despite breeding so many different kinds of animals, however, the only animal experiments that Victor performed were aimed at trying to develop a germ-free mouse. His plan involved birthing "clean" mice via cesarean section and then guarding the young against contaminants, a practice common today in animal research facilities. Victor even designed and built a special mouse cage with openings for his hands, and crafted a little operating table inside the cage.

During World War II, the U.S. government ordered a million mice from Tumblebrook Farm to test a potential vaccine against malaria. Before the order could be filled, the atomic bomb ended the war, but Victor remained optimistic about the brave new world of laboratory animal breeding. He reasoned that scientists not only would continue needing the animals he'd been providing all along but also would want other, more novel medical models, too, as research studies grew more sophisticated. Victor created the West Foundation, named for his wife's family, with the sole purpose of conducting "a systematic search for such animals that might provide medical research with new experimental models."

Victor knew that for animals to be truly useful for researchers, they would have to be small, easily handled, prolific, and easy keepers—that is, creatures that ate little, bred quickly, adapted easily to different climates, and were hardy enough to survive the rigors of being transported from one place to another. Along the way to discovering the gerbil—an animal that nicely fit this list of criteria—Victor bred cotton rats, snowball rats, meadow voles, white-footed mice, wood rats, red-backed mice, jumping mice, short-tailed shrews, Chinese hamsters, rice rats, pine mice, lemming mice, long-tailed shrews, pocket mice, kangaroo rats, grasshopper mice, harvest mice, Philippine tree shrews, banana rats, and bandicoots.

Victor marketed each of his new finds to laboratory researchers and breeders by mailing them thick manila folders containing press releases and photographs. He shared these with my father while we were in Kansas, who in turn showed them to us. These folders were like the media kits that Hollywood agents send out for the movie stars they represent. The folders each bore the bold headline "Announcing . . ." followed by the name of the animal, with a photographic portrait taken against an appropriate creative backdrop. The Chinese hamster's portrait, for instance, was shot against a Chinese screen, along with a Chinese doll sporting a broad-brimmed hat and long white beard.

With his zeal for providing the healthiest, highest-quality laboratory animals possible, Victor earned a solid reputation among researchers and other breeders. And with more than forty men working for him at Tumblebrook Farm, Victor also ranked as the largest employer in the Brant Lake area.

By adventuring around the world, starting his own business from the ground up, studying exotic animals, and ultimately freeing himself from depending on anyone else for a livelihood, Victor Schwentker was everything that my father aspired to be.

~

THE first written mention of gerbils was in 1866 by Father Armand David, a French missionary priest, when he sent what he called "yellow rats" from northern China to the Museum of Natural History in Paris. The scientist Alphonse Milne-Edwards named these gerbils *Meriones unguiculatus* a year later; this Latin name means "clawed warrior" in English and is derived in part from the name of the Greek warrior Meriones.

Nobody knows how Victor Schwentker first learned about gerbils. Given his steady consumption of newspapers, books, magazines, and scientific journals, it was probably through reading. At any rate, Victor received his first shipment of gerbils from Japanese scientists in 1954 and promptly produced his usual promotional packet. The original black-and-white portrait on this publicity folder is of a gerbil standing on its hind legs, its long, silky tufted tail shown to best advantage. The gerbil appears to be reading the enormous book in front of it, which is titled *A Natural History of Central Asia*, volume XI: *The Mammals of China and Mongolia, Central Asiatic Expeditions*.

Inside the packet, the promotional literature is heady, almost giddy. The gerbil's many virtues—friendliness, curiosity, smarts, environmental adaptability—made Victor rave, "Of all the animals that have been introduced as potentially useful experimental animals, perhaps the most remarkable has been the Mongolian gerbil."

Victor wrote those words at the end of 1967, precisely when my own father first contacted him for more information about breeding gerbils from our apartment in Fort Leavenworth. The two men exchanged several letters and agreed to meet early in 1968. By then, Victor was nearly seventy years old, and he'd been hoping to find someone to take over his gerbil colony, the last of his laboratory animals.

My father, meanwhile, was growing increasingly disillusioned with military life and with the country's involvement in Vietnam. "I can't believe this," he'd say at least once during every nightly television newscast, as the body count rose. "They have to know this war is a mistake. How can they not? We should really do something."

"Like what?" Mom would say, coming into the living room and shaking her head at the TV as if it were to blame for the state of our country. "We have to support the war. We're military."

Dad must have expressed some of his reservations about

military life to Victor, for in a letter dated December 4, 1967, Victor wrote:

> *You have said that you do not expect to get rich raising gerbils. In view of the fact that you chose the Navy as a career, I am justified in assuming that you never expected to get rich. "Comfortable" is, in my opinion, a much better state of finances, and I would like to predict that a properly operated gerbil colony will bring you an income of ten to twelve thousand dollars per year.*

This may not sound like much today. But in the 1960s, and added to my father's pension when he retired from the Navy, it was such a princely sum that Dad used his red pencil to underline these heartening words as he read Victor's letter to us.

He flew out to see Victor in Brant Lake shortly after that, and the two men sealed their deal. Victor agreed to let my father have his business, including the name Tumblebrook Farm, for $60,000. Dad planned to buy his own farm after he got his orders and knew where we were headed after Kansas. Once we were moved in, he would gradually move Victor's breeding stock of gerbils and his equipment to our own plot of land. Dad didn't have $60,000, but that didn't seem to bother Victor: in a gentleman's agreement, the two men shook hands and Victor agreed to let my father pay him back over time. They were both that sure of Dad's success in the gerbil-farming business.

Chapter Eight

Who's Going to Marry Her Now?

The Pony Club

CREDIT THE HOLLY ROBINSON COLLECTION

One chilly winter night, Dad announced at the dinner table that he wanted to read us some fan letters he'd gotten in response to his latest *Science News* article just as Mom was serving dessert, a new chocolate cake recipe from the *I Hate to Cook* cookbook.

"The beauty of this cake was that it was made in one bowl," Mom said, ignoring Dad when he snapped the first letter free from its envelope with an eye-catching shake. "You just make three wells in the center of the dry ingredients for the oil, the eggs, and the milk," she continued. "There's really no mess at all."

Making recipes from *I Hate to Cook* was almost as easy as cooking with Campbell's soup, her other favorite no-fuss mealtime helper, Mom added. "I think this will become my kitchen bible."

Dad cleared his throat and waved the letter in front of us. "This letter came to me from Delbert D. Thiessen, Ph.D., assistant chairman of the Department of Psychology at the University of Texas in Austin," he announced. He repeated the man's name and title to be sure that we were as impressed as he was.

"You know," Mom told him, "I worked hard on this dinner. You haven't said a thing about it."

Dad looked bewildered. "But I love everything you cook. You know that."

"Still." My mother lit a cigarette and pushed her own cake aside, untouched. The gauntlet was thrown. "You might at least acknowledge what I do around here. I'm your wife, not your slave. I don't care how many gerbils you've got in that goddamn basement. I don't want to hear about them *anymore*." With that, she rose from the table and disappeared into her bedroom, slamming the door behind her.

Donald, Gail, and I took this as a cue that we could eat our cake in the den in front of the TV. We stood up and gathered our plates, but Dad stopped us. "Wait," he said. "Sit down. You haven't been excused yet."

Gail ran off, as defiant as ever. But Donald and I sat down again and made faces at each other across the table while Dad, oblivious to our antics, shared the letter from Dr. Thiessen in Austin, Texas.

Dear Commander Robinson:

I read with great interest your article appearing in Science News *on the epileptic gerbil. It was well done and informative. . . . We are attempting to work out the genetic mechanism for seizing and relate the effect to changes in blood sugar levels. Much hormone work is complete and will be written up for publications soon. I produced a film on gerbil behavior, part of which is scheduled for presentation this summer on an NBC program entitled* Animal Secrets. *In any case, work goes on. . . . As the studies crystallize, I'll pass them on.*

Dad put the letter down and looked at Donald and me. "There, kids, what do you think of that? Gerbils on NBC!"

"That's great, Dad," I said. I had to say something.

"May we please be excused, Daddy, sir?" Donald asked.

We raced each other to the television when Dad granted us permission, leaving our father alone at the table with his letter and cigarette and one-bowl chocolate cake.

I WAS plain-looking, with a nose that would have been ordinary, except for the slight bump that remained after the newspaper delivery boy ran me over with his bicycle in Virginia. Not ugly, just unexceptional: I had an average sort of mouth, brown hair, and brown eyes with no hints of green or gold in them like the characters in the books I read. As if these utterly average looks weren't enough to bear, I also had a snaggle tooth. One of my incisors had grown in crooked and ridged because my mother had contracted German measles during her pregnancy with me.

Kids teased me about the tooth in elementary school enough so that I knew to smile with my lips closed. Nonetheless, there were those who noticed and remarked upon it in junior high at Fort Leavenworth, making junior high even more of a hell than it already was. In many ways, it was a hell devised by teenagers caught between rebelling and serving their parents, the way their parents served the country. The dances were the sort where the girls wore party dresses and stood on one side of the gym, miserably waiting for some brazen male to cross the great divide and ask them to dance; at my first such dance, I wore a pale blue gauzy dress with a bow in the back and, of course, a snow-white Peter Pan collar; I looked like a minister's wife. I came home ecstatic because I'd been asked to dance exactly once, by a boy whose collar was whiter than mine.

Meanwhile, various factions of the kids I went to school with were rebelling against Vietnam, so our teachers at General George S. Patton Jr. Junior High School did their best to maintain order in true Army fashion. Each morning, they lined us up in the cafeteria for inspection. Our skirts were to be no more than two inches above the knee; our bangs couldn't touch our eyebrows; and girls were not allowed to wear makeup, heels, or dangling earrings. Naturally, these rules only provoked certain girls to roll up their skirts in the bathrooms, apply lipstick, and shake off their barrettes and hairbands the minute inspection was over.

Among my Army brat classmates, I was already an outcast for having a father who was in the Navy. And, of course, Dad had that secret stash of gerbils keeping him basement-bound for reasons I could never reveal. I reacted to both the kids and the Army by becoming a pacifist and carrying a photograph of my horse, Ladybug, in a locket around my neck. There was no point in trying to fit in, so I might as well do what I wanted.

By eighth grade I was a good enough rider to join the Pony Club, a group of riders who followed the more expert hunter-jumpers during Sunday morning fox hunts. The hunts were thrilling; we'd gallop through dew-heavy fields and along winding wooded trails, ducking low tree branches as we followed on the hocks of more experienced riders who careened over stone walls, ditches, and wooden fences. People were always being tossed off when their horses refused the jumps and scrambling out of the way of the horses galloping and leaping behind them. Occasionally, a horse dumped its rider and cantered merrily back to the barn with reins dangling and stirrups flapping. All of this was accompanied by the frantic baying of beagles following the scented trail laid ahead of time by one of the Hunt Club members, and by the trumpeting of a brass horn blown by our hunt master, a flamingo of a man with a skeletal build and a scarlet coat.

The stable was my sanctuary, the one place where I felt comfortable in my own skin. But there was school to contend with, still, during all of those other hours. I was never asked to a sleepover or a party, and lately I had been longing to be not like Trixie Belden, girl detective, but like Lisa Agnew, the most beautiful girl at General George S. Patton Jr. Junior High School.

Lisa Agnew had blue eyes, a straight nose, and sleek blond hair parted in the middle that swung shut like a pair of curtains on either side of her oval face. Her teeth were straight and white, and she wore empire-waist, low-necked shirred dresses that emphasized her full breasts. Most impressive of all, she had a boyfriend in high school who took her on dates in his own car. I held my breath each time Lisa passed me in the hall, longing for her to notice me and terrified that she might.

And then, suddenly, Lisa was gone. She was absent from

school for so long that I was certain her father must have been transferred; like Virginia, our Fort Leavenworth classes were always gaining and losing students without warning. But Lisa returned after a time, transformed by an ugly red scar across her face.

"What happened to you?" I breathed when I came into the girls' bathroom later that morning and discovered Lisa there, alone, leaning toward the mirror to cake more forbidden makeup onto her scar.

"My boyfriend crashed his car," she said flatly.

I nearly wept for her. "But you'll get better, won't you?" I asked. "The scar will fade."

Lisa eyed me in the mirror with pity. "Obviously, you've never known what it's like to be beautiful."

It would be many, many years before I'd be able to look into a mirror without seeing the ghost of Lisa's face next to mine, measuring what she had lost and what I would never have.

GRADUALLY, I was spending less time at home and more time at the stables with the older teenagers who entered horse shows, that strange breed of competitive, no-nonsense child who spends hours working on perfect form during the posting trot. These were the kids Mom didn't want me to ride with because she thought I wasn't experienced enough.

"Those daredevils are always racing around like crazy on the trails and taking jumps they have no business taking," she warned. "Don't you dare go out with them, Holly."

Ah, but what's a mother's dare to a thirteen-year-old girl

but a summons, a battle cry, a gauntlet thrown? Out I went, riding with the older kids every day after school and earning their tolerance, if not respect. I might not be beautiful, but I could keep up on the trails.

And then, during one furiously fast ride, I decided to follow one of my new teenage friends over a high wooden gate on a trail that paralleled a paved road. Ladybug and I had taken higher jumps in the ring; I knew all it would take was a jab of my heels to make the horse go faster and rising in my saddle at the right moment while thrusting my hands forward to give Ladybug enough rein to sail clear of the fence.

My friend took the jump first. Then I kicked my heels into Ladybug's dappled gray sides and we were off. I pushed my hands forward and rose out of the saddle to meet the jump. I did everything exactly as my instructor, a retired general, had taught me during endless drills in the ring.

But Ladybug did not. She didn't like the sight of that jump or the feel of me leaving the saddle. She didn't want to be there at all. The grain was probably being dumped into her feed bucket back at the stables *right that minute*. So my horse veered sharply away from the fence and bucked, dislodging me from the saddle like a catapult launching a pumpkin.

I don't remember much of what happened after that. I woke up alone on the paved road and discovered that my horse and friend were gone. A hot, salty liquid filled my mouth, running down my throat and choking me. I spat it out. There was more blood than I'd ever seen, and it was still pouring out of my mouth and nose. The metallic smell and taste of my own blood filled the air.

I tried to stand up, but my legs were too weak. I sank down beside the road and passed out again.

Max was the one who found me. He was one of the military prisoners who worked in the stables during his parole, a skinny, dark-haired guy whom all of the girls loved to flirt with. He'd been in the barn when Ladybug came cantering home and dashed into her stall wearing her tack, followed shortly by the terrified teenager who had been riding ahead of me. She told Max where to find me. Unlike our parents, we all trusted the prisoners completely, because they talked to us as if we weren't children.

Max had no access to a car, so he climbed onto the tractor he used to pull the hay wagon. He drove it as fast as he could to the jump, where he found me lying beside the road, barely conscious. Max picked me up and laid me gently down on top of the hay, then drove me back to the barn.

~

I'D LOST seven teeth, I'd broken my nose, and my face was so swollen that I could feel my cheeks on my shirt collar without turning my head. I'd been wearing a riding helmet, luckily, so my skull was intact. But nobody would give me a mirror.

Donald and my father drove to the jump and tried to find my teeth, but they were too smashed to be reset in my mouth. I came home from the hospital with nothing but stitches where the oral surgeon had removed the last tiny fragments of shattered teeth pressed into my gums by the fall. I lay on the couch, head pounding, sore and drowsy with pain medication.

I turned onto my side and pressed my throbbing face

against the pillows. "At least my snaggletooth is gone!" I yelled into the kitchen, but neither of my parents heard me. They were too busy arguing about Ladybug.

"I knew that horse was a bad idea from the start," Dad insisted. "We should shoot it. I should personally load up my old Navy pistol and go down there and goddamn shoot that goddamn horse."

"It's not the horse's fault," Mom said. "I told Holly not to jump. She disobeyed. There's nothing wrong with that horse. Nobody's going to shoot it. It would break Holly's heart, losing Ladybug. That horse is her only friend in the world."

"Jesus Christ, Sally!" Dad yelled. "Look at Holly. Just look at her! Who's going to marry her now?"

Chapter Nine

My Sister the Time Traveler

Gail feeding our gerbils

CREDIT: D. G. ROBINSON JR.

In every family there are labels, and you spend most of your life trying to rip them off. In ours, my father was stern, Mom was fun, I was smart, Donald was wild, and Gail was beautiful. Those labels defined our default modes, the roles we played over and over again, and made us think that we understood one another even when we were itching to escape our own skins.

My sister, Gail, like my mother, was born beautiful and had an air of expectation about her, an attitude that the world was there for her pleasure. I was too good a child to ever say that I hated her, but I seethed at times, staring in the mirror at my plain face topped by its boyish haircut. It was hardly fair that nature should grant Gail all of the goods.

I longed to have my sister's heart-shaped face, those dimples, the blond ringlets, those bottomless dark eyes with their long black princess eyelashes. She was so beautiful, "such a cunning child, just like my little Sally," as Grandmother Keach said, that even Donald didn't tease her. In families with three children, there is usually an odd man out, and that was me.

Donald and Gail teamed up to play together in ways that I could never be with either of them.

Despite her princess-doll looks and forest-fairy grin, Gail was fearless, dogging Donald's heels in Virginia whenever he went down to the lake to muck around for minnows and painted turtles and frogs. In that way, too, Gail was like my mother. Mom was so brave that she'd run away from home on the family pony, bareback and without a bridle, when she was just four years old. My mother made it two miles down the road before a neighbor spotted her trotting away and took her back home. Who knows how Mom mounted the pony? She probably charmed him the way Gail hypnotized our dogs, who always slept alongside Gail when she colored on the floor and let her do terrible things to their ears and tails. Even our old fox terrier, Tip the Terrible, never bit her.

For all of her childish beauty, energy, and mischief, though, Gail suffered infections frequently as a toddler and was often short of breath. She huffed and puffed when she ran down the hallway after us. She had to stop and gasp for air if she tried to keep up with Donald or the dogs, who always waited patiently for her to catch up.

Dad accepted this. "You know Gail's just doing that to get attention," he'd say whenever Mom worried aloud that something might be wrong. "The youngest kid always has to work hardest to get noticed."

But my mother persisted. In Virginia, she began taking Gail to every military doctor who agreed to see her. Most shook their heads and called my sister's mysterious condition "a failure to thrive." Finally, Mom defied them all, and my father, too, by paying to see an outside doctor, a specialist who finally gave her an answer. It wasn't one she wanted. The last year we lived in Virginia, Gail was diagnosed with cystic fibrosis. She was three years old.

The body of someone with cystic fibrosis produces too much mucus. Children with the disease suffer chronic infections because the mucus in their lungs is so thick that it clogs the respiratory system and allows bacteria to grow. The extra sticky mucus also clogs the pancreas, undermining digestion.

In this country, cystic fibrosis is the most common fatal hereditary disease among Caucasian children; one out of every twenty Caucasians carries the recessive gene for it. Probability dictates that one out of every four children born to carrier parents will have the disease. Medical treatments have come a long way since my sister was diagnosed; today, people with cystic fibrosis can live into their thirties, or even their forties.

We were stunned. None of us had ever heard of cystic fibrosis, and there had never been a case of it on either side of the family. There followed several brief but hostile volleys between my parents, each furiously accusing the other of having a bum gene in the family tree. Then Dad went to sea again, leaving Mom to cope alone with finding Gail whatever treatments were available.

Gail was a stoic, though, and Donald and I often forgot that she was sick at all. In Virginia, and even during our first year in Kansas, she was able to cheerfully run after us and chattered incessantly whenever she could catch her breath.

"Can you eat chocolate, Grandmother?" Gail asked Grandmother Keach one day.

"Yes," said Grandmother. "I love chocolate."

Gail beamed. "Me too!" She wrinkled her nose. "Do you wheeze and cough sometimes, too, Grandmother?"

Grandmother nodded. "I have asthma," she said. "It's not always easy for me to breathe."

"You know what? I can't breathe sometimes, either! Look what happens!" Gail crowed, and ran up and down the hallway to make herself cough and wheeze, skidding in her socks just the way Donald and I had taught her.

~

BY THE time we moved to Fort Leavenworth, Gail was almost four years old. Despite having occasional bouts of pneumonia and even being hospitalized for it, she was a terror. She poked straw into my horse's nostril to see what Ladybug would do, tore up Donald's homework when he wouldn't play with her, and got into my Barbies, cutting their hair with nail scissors and tearing apart their clothes. I was almost too old to play with Barbies, but I resented the fact that Gail could do anything she liked and still be praised for her beauty by everyone who saw her.

Just before leaving Virginia for Kansas, Gail had started sleeping in an oxygen tent, a pale blue sheet of plastic draped over her bed and attached to a humming metal tank. The tent collected droplets of moisture inside it, and Gail crawled out of her mist tent each morning with her fine hair in tight curls about her scalp, making her look more like a pale, ethereal fairy than ever. Sometimes I fantasized that I could sleep in her tent and wake up looking like that. Most of the time, though, I ignored my sister, glad that my legs and lungs could carry me out of our apartment and off to the stables.

Mom was becoming increasingly consumed with Gail's care. She gave Gail physical therapy exercises and medication, and tried to protect my sister from the infectious diseases that other children in the neighborhood might bring into the house; Donald and I were seldom allowed to bring friends to the apartment. The most I saw of my mother during that time was at the stables, for she continued to ride despite being pregnant again. Our last rides together were in late spring, when the violets were starting to bloom along our favorite bridle trail, a narrow, tree-canopied path so lush with giant ferns that it was easy to imagine dinosaurs roaming there at night. Not surprisingly, my mother seemed depressed, overwhelmed by both her unexpected pregnancy and taking care of Gail.

Once, Mom grew so exasperated with my nitwit chatter that she scolded me as we headed out on one of our favorite trails. "You're going to kill yourself on that horse one of these days, because you never pay attention when you're riding," she said as I swiveled in my saddle to start talking to her.

"I am not!" I protested, still facing backward. Just then, Ladybug darted beneath a steel guy wire that ran from a telephone pole to the ground, knocking me clear out of the saddle. My mother laughed, so the fall was worth it.

What I didn't know was that Mom was deliberately, defiantly riding her horse during this pregnancy over the protests of my father, her friends, and even her own doctor. She wanted to lose the baby.

"I just wanted a delicate little miscarriage," she confessed to me years later. "I didn't think I could face another child being sick like Gail. I didn't believe I was strong enough to go through that again."

Dad, for his part, left Gail's nursing to Mom and retreated deeper and deeper into his mysterious basement world, or brought the gerbils upstairs to photograph them. In 1969, he published two articles in the magazine *Highlights for Children,* this time using the byline "D. G. Robinson Jr., Member, American Association of Laboratory Animals." The first, published in January, introduced gerbils as "friendly desert jumpers" and offered a fetching portrait of a gerbil sitting comfortably in one of my dad's slippers.

The second piece appeared in October of that year and was a child's guide to gerbil care; it included, in abbreviated form, the mimeographed experiments that Marcy and I had tried doing in our Virginia garage. To illustrate one experiment about comparing a gerbil's heart rate to your own, there was a photograph in *Highlights for Children* of Donald and me that Dad had taken in the living room of our Fort Leavenworth apartment. My mother had dressed both of us in neatly ironed button-down shirts for that photo, and Donald is valiantly positioning an enormous stethoscope on the jittery rodent I'm clutching in my hand.

When Dad showed us the magazine, I remembered the rapid flutter of the terrified animal's heartbeat beneath my fingers, and how amazing it was to feel tangible proof that a fragile little thing like a heart was powerful enough to keep any animal alive.

Donald and I often talked about death, a subject our parents would leave the room to avoid, but my brother and I never discussed the possibility of Gail dying. In the way of children, we talked about what scared us most by playing a game that involved asking each other what death we'd choose.

The one who could think of the most dramatic death ever—being set on fire while being tossed out of an airplane into a sea of sharks, for instance—won.

It was around that time that I suddenly began wishing for a religion, any religion. But Dad maintained that he was a "confirmed agnostic" and wouldn't take us to church, and my mother said she was too busy to spend her Sundays praying somewhere else when she could pray right at home. So I went with friends to the Catholic church, and horrified my parents by wearing a silver cross and asking to be confirmed a Catholic. I had no idea what that meant. I only knew that I wanted to believe in a heaven that would have sunlit, lily-covered ponds with white winged horses grazing nearby, and angels with more gauzy gowns than Barbie.

EVERY now and then, our family spent a day together in Kansas, usually on a Sunday, when Dad would take us on rides through the rolling Kansas hills in his new car. This was a Buick that my brother called the "Station Wagon of Death" because of the way Dad liked to gun the engine up hills, shouting "Here we go, kids!" just before we went airborne at the crest of each one.

Otherwise, I hardly saw my brother. Donald showed little interest in horses after our new gelding, Reveille, reared and toppled over on him, pinning him like a deer beneath Godzilla. While I spent time at the stables, he was devoted to his new chemistry set, which had arrived in the mail with its own alcohol lamp. I always knew when Donald was home by the smoke and bad smells oozing out from beneath the closed door of his bedroom. Whenever he did leave the house, Donald ran with a small gang of like-minded boys to shoot guns, ride bikes, and play around the foxholes near the soldiers doing drills with grenades.

"That kid is always somewhere he shouldn't be," Mom would sigh.

One night, Dad retreated to his basement gerbilry after dinner, as usual, and Donald ran outside to see a friend's new bike. It was autumn but still hot, the thick air barely stirring beneath the ceiling fans. Mom was doing dishes when suddenly she shook her hands dry and, leaving the pans in the sink, retreated to the couch and curled up with one of her science fiction novels and a cigarette. She didn't light the cigarette, though; she just held it between her fingers and stared at it, as if wondering what it was, resting her elbow on her pregnant belly to see the cigarette in front of her. It was an unnerving moment; my mother never sat still.

"Want me to help you finish in the kitchen, Mom?" I asked.

"I want you to do your sister's exercises," Mom said. "I'm not up to it tonight."

Gail's exercises involved laying my skinny little sister across the big gold corduroy pillow on Mom's bed in ten different positions, all of them uncomfortable. Many required Gail to dangle upside down like a broken doll. You had to pound the mucus out of her lungs by smacking one cupped hand across the brittle bones of her rib cage. As primitive as this treatment seemed, it was effective in getting the mucus to drain.

In Virginia, Gail had been relatively compliant about her

medicine, the mist tent, and the never-ending thumping exercises. Now that she was four years old, however, Gail recognized that Donald and I never underwent such torture. She had begun to resist and complain.

"She won't let me," I said automatically, not because I thought this was true, but because I was so taken aback that my mother would ask me to do this. Despite the difference in our ages, I continued to resent Gail while worrying about her at the same time and feeling guilty for loving her any less than unconditionally. I couldn't help it, though. Gail could do whatever she wanted and get away with it because she could play her mortality card.

"You have to make her let you do them," Mom said. "I need you to."

I sighed and went to find my sister.

Gail was standing in my room, feet wide apart, a Barbie doll in each hand, like King Kong ready for a helicopter attack. She grinned like the devil when she saw me.

"Mom says I have to do your exercises," I said.

"No!" she shrieked. "No, no, no!"

"I don't want to do them, either. But if you let me put you over the pillow and do them, I'll let you keep holding my Barbies. And I'll tell you a story, too," I said.

Gail agreed. I followed her down the hallway to my mother's bedroom, where Gail managed to climb onto the bed while still clutching the Barbies. My sister flopped herself down over the gold pillow, head dangling.

I'd watched my mother do the exercises often enough to know what to do. Still, I felt as ungainly and evil as an ogre, with my huge hand on Gail's fragile body. I felt ashamed of how much I'd resented her when this was what she had to look forward to every day. Somehow the reality of hitting her hadn't hit me until I had to take part.

Just as I was working up to feeling out-and-out pity for my sister, Gail cracked the heads of my Barbies together. "A story!" she yelled.

"Okay, okay," I said. "But no wrecking my dolls."

"You're too old for dolls." Gail giggled. "You wear a bra."

"You'll wear a bra someday, too," I said, and then bit my lip, because I didn't believe my own lie, and I knew by her silence that Gail didn't, either. After a minute of punishing quiet punctuated only by the thump of my hand on my sister's body, I began, "The hero of my story is a little girl like you," I said, "with blond hair and dark eyes. But she's a magic girl."

"And her name is Gail!" Gail guessed.

"That's right," I agreed. "But this little girl is always nice to her big sister."

"She is not."

"Yes, she is. And you know what? This little Gail can fly, too, and she has so many magical powers that even dragons are afraid of her."

After that first night, my mother began asking me to do Gail's exercises more often. To help Gail pass the time, I read to her from my books, holding them in my free hand and reading loudly over the steady popping rhythm of my cupped palm. Our favorite was *A Wrinkle in Time* by Madeline L'Engle. L'Engle used mind-bending words that intrigued us both, such as *gamboled,* and Gail and I loved to imagine *tessering,* L'Engle's word for traveling through time. The book introduced us to concepts and questions that kept our minds buzzing for hours.

We wondered if we could find a tesseract, too, and travel through a dark nothingness to a different place and time.

I especially identified with Meg Murry, the book's main character, who had "mouse brown hair" like mine and felt like an outcast at school. Gail's favorite character was Meg's little brother, Charles Wallace, who was, like Gail, four years old and different from everyone else. Meg and Charles even had parents like ours.

"Meg looked up at her mother," I read to Gail one night, "half in loving admiration, half in sullen resentment." Meg's mother, writes L'Engle, has "flaming red hair, creamy skin, and violet eyes with long dark lashes," all of which "seemed even more spectacular in comparison with Meg's outrageous plainness." And Meg's father was missing. Granted, Mr. Murry was actually physically trapped on another planet, but ours might as well have been.

~

THE end, when it came, was swift. It was late August when Gail was admitted to the hospital with another bout of pneumonia. I was at a friend's house when I was called home early.

I went into the living room and found my father and brother sitting on the couch. My mother, now enormously pregnant with whoever would join our family next, was curled up in the brown wing chair in the living room and looked, except for that big belly, like a little child. She was crying. I'd never seen my mother cry before.

My father sat with his hands dangling helplessly between his knees. He simply told Donald and me the facts. *Gail. Hos-*

pital. Didn't make it this time. "We're sorry, kids," he said. "Very, very sorry."

He snapped his fingers to show us how mercilessly quick a life can end. For a while, that was the only sound in the room, a damp echo of my father's thumb against his finger as his Navy ring flashed bright blue and gold.

My parents seldom spoke of Gail again, after donating her body to research and holding a small memorial service in Kansas. When I thought about Gail, I comforted myself by imagining that she'd left us behind by tessering through a wrinkle in time into another dimension. I longed to follow her through that dark nothingness to a far-flung planet where many-armed, furry beasts could warm us and heal us after such a long, hard journey.

Chapter Ten

Welcome to the Poor Farm

The poor farm in winter

CREDIT: THE HOLLY ROBINSON COLLECTION

We left Kansas for our new home in Massachusetts sixteen months later, in December 1969. I was sandwiched between my brother Donald and little Philip in his elbow-cracking plastic car seat. The windows were closed because of the cold, and my parents smoked with such relentless abandon that I glanced up from my book at one point and thought we were driving through fog. When it was too dark to read, I stared over the front seat at the headlights rolling like white beads over the hilly landscape and increasing in number as we drew closer to the East Coast. Meanwhile, the red ends of my parents' cigarettes danced like fireflies above the dashboard.

Nobody spoke of what we'd left behind. My parents were brokenhearted, but they were military. They were also busy with a new baby: scarcely two weeks after Gail's death, my brother Philip had been born, a robust baby who weighed over eight pounds. The nurses had to physically break my mother's water during childbirth because she had a double membrane.

"You weren't ever going to lose that baby, darling," one nurse told her, "no matter what you did."

I had turned fourteen just two weeks before packing up

my room in Kansas to leave. Donald was eleven years old and still needed more action than he got. On our cross-country drive, he'd reach across Philip to give me an Indian burn on the arm or punch the top of my leg whenever he was bored, which was most of the time, and I'd punch him back. By the end of our first full day of driving, bruises bloomed along our thighs. We couldn't escape each other or do much else because we were wedged into place. Dad's combination of military efficiency and pack rat mentality meant that we were prepared for every possible emergency; at the last minute, he'd even insisted on stocking up at the Fort Leavenworth commissary.

"You never know when we'll need food," he told my mother.

Mom rolled her eyes. "We've got enough canned goods in this car to survive a nuclear war," she said.

We had also packed our pets. Dad had sold his basement stock of gerbils to a pet store in Kansas City, but we had brought Samantha, a Siamese cat, and Beau, a black miniature poodle. The cat howled continuously from her travel crate tucked among the boxes in the back of the station wagon, and the poodle kept trying to scrabble over the rear seat like a drowning passenger from the *Titanic* after the last departing lifeboat. Beau was a strong case for pet Prozac; he was so anxious that he chewed on the dashboard of the car anytime we left him unattended. By the time we reached Massachusetts, the metal bones of the dashboard were emerging from the last tattered bits of plastic skin.

More than once on that trip, Mom referred to us as the "Fort Leavenworth hillbillies." "The only thing we don't have in this car is a banjo," she said. But Dad drove silently and steadily forward, a cigarette tucked into one corner of his mouth, only occasionally swerving as he reached behind the seat to swat Donald at sixty miles per hour.

~

MY FATHER had flown to Massachusetts a few months before our departure from Kansas and bought our new home without any of us seeing it first. His new orders were to head up the Naval Science Department at the U.S. Merchant Marine Academy in Kings Point, Long Island, but Mom wouldn't let him move us to New York State. She used me as an excuse. At fourteen, I was "getting to be quite the handful," she pronounced. "Just the right age to get into Trouble with those merchant Marines." (Whenever Mom said "trouble" as if it were capitalized, I knew she meant "pregnant.")

Dad agreed to commute, spending only weekends with us while completing his final two years in the Navy to earn his twenty-year pension. He'd had it with military life, he told us. He couldn't support the war in Vietnam and didn't want to travel his entire life. He was disappointed that his last assignment was a teaching post rather than something more active. On the bright side, this would give him a chance to buy a farm and start his gerbil empire. His plan to make it as a gerbil farmer was still largely in his own mind, perhaps because if he had tried to describe it to us, there would have been mutiny. All we knew was that Mom was finally getting her farm.

Dad had considered buying property close to Victor Schwentker's in Brant Lake, New York. But my mother, with raw memories of living in rural Maine as a child, nixed this idea when she discovered that the wind chill factor in Brant

Lake could send temperatures plummeting to fifty degrees below zero. Dad sought another location within a reasonable drive of an international airport—an important feature, given that his plan involved shipping gerbils all over the world. Mom had relatives in Massachusetts, so he finally settled on Bradley International Airport outside of Hartford, Connecticut, as his gerbil epicenter. He searched for an affordable farm in a steadily expanding radius from there, and at last found what he wanted in West Brookfield, Massachusetts.

We exited the Massachusetts Turnpike in Sturbridge and took a back road off a back road off a back road. It was midafternoon, two weeks before Christmas, and snow was falling in lazy, moth-sized flakes.

"Isn't this great?" Dad asked, maneuvering the Station Wagon of Death around another slick, hairpin turn. "This place isn't even on the way to anywhere."

"You sure know how to pick 'em," Mom said, lighting another cigarette.

West Brookfield looked like a storybook village, with a classic town common complete with a bandstand and brightly lit Christmas tree. Dad had already studied up on local history; now he launched into tour guide mode to drum up enthusiasm among his flagging troops.

"This is one of the oldest towns in New England," he said. "That Congregational church traces its history back to the Quaboag Plantation in 1717. What do you think of that, kids?"

We troops were silent. As we coasted through the center of town, Dad pointed out Ye Olde Tavern, a rambling white house with black shutters, and said it was the second-oldest tavern in Massachusetts, with wood buildings dating back to

1760. "Town taverns were the center of Colonial life," he marveled. "George Washington stayed right here at this one, during the very first year of his presidency in 1789. President John Adams stayed here, too. I can't believe this tavern is still serving meals, can you?"

Gloomily, I stared through the windshield, shoulders hunched and arms folded tightly against my body to ward off any unexpected attacks from Donald, who at the moment was busy unraveling threads from Philip's favorite blanket while Philip watched, silent and wide-eyed.

We circled around town to view a tiny stone library, a big white town hall, a diner, a drugstore, and several more churches as Dad continued his schoolboy report. The lone sour note was a state marker on Route 9 commemorating the deaths of the first settlers "On Indian Lands Called Quabaug. Attacked by Indians in 1675." This monument, Dad told us somberly, was erected in memory of settlers slaughtered during King Philip's War.

"The Indians attacked every one of Massachusetts's eight towns along the Connecticut River," he said. "Many of the settlers who survived fled the area entirely."

I wanted to follow them. My father was right: West Brookfield wasn't even on the way to anywhere! Not a movie theater or swimming pool or cute Army soldier in sight. Resentment sat in my throat, thick and hot.

"I'm bored," I announced.

"Bored? How can you be bored?" Dad chided. "There's so much to see! And it's all new! This is our new home! It's exciting!"

"You're just tired," Mom said. "We're all tired." She gave my father a look, and he stopped talking.

We crossed the broad, half-frozen Quaboag River on a two-lane bridge that rattled beneath the car. From there we made a steep ascent along the aptly named Long Hill Road. At the crest of the hill, overlooking a sloping field across the street that seemed to plunge straight into the silver ribbon of the Quaboag River far below, sat our new home, a Gothic Revival farmhouse with a military-green paint job that emphasized its stern, square shoulders.

"This house looks like a prison," I said.

"It's a classic," Dad protested. "An antique."

"What are those things on the doors?" Donald asked.

"Hex signs," Mom answered immediately. She knew about things like witches and psychics and astrology and aliens. I noticed that she was sitting up straighter in her seat, staring at the house.

"Are hex signs good or bad if they're on a house?" Donald asked. He was kicking my mother's seat, which ordinarily would have made her yell.

"They're meant to protect your house from evil spirits," Mom said.

"It doesn't look like they're working," I said. "This place is a dump."

Dad slowed the car to let us take a good long look at our future. Set above the road on a small rise, the huge house towered above the car, its tiny windows squinting down at us. Across the river, I could make out a row of crooked wooden buildings that once had been shoe and box factories, derelict remains of an industrial age that had relied on railroads and boats to move goods from here along the Quaboag River to Boston.

"The good thing," Mom said at last, "is that this place has to be better on the inside than it looks from out here."

"Not necessarily," I said.

"Maybe it's haunted," Donald said.

"Maybe you're stupid," I said.

Dad pulled into the driveway, where a hearse was parked in front of the carport. "Well," he said, stubbing his cigarette out into the ashtray, "that's something."

"There has to be an explanation," Mom said.

We all sat there looking at the hearse and trying to think of one. There was a small symphony of sounds in the car: Philip sucking on his pacifier, Donald kicking at the seat, the anxious panting of the poodle, and the occasional pitiful howl from the Siamese. Dad and Mom each smoked another cigarette as we continued to stare at the hearse. It was painted a grayish purple color not yet named by man, and it had hex signs and flowers all over it.

"Okay," Dad declared at last with a smart, military tap on the steering wheel. "I'm going in. You stay here and guard the car. There's probably some damn flower children camped in our house."

"Hippies," Mom agreed. The low opinion of dirty hippies held by both of my parents was one of the most enduring bonds of their marriage.

I pressed my face closer to the window, watching Dad approach the house full tilt in true Navy officer style, knees high, arms pumping to propel himself through the deep snow around the house to a door I couldn't see.

Hippies! This was the most thrilling possibility that had been presented to me in two thousand miles. On Fort Leavenworth, there weren't any hippies—they probably would have been shot on sight—but I knew all about them. I was only fourteen, but I would have hitchhiked to Woodstock that August if my mother hadn't threatened to sell my horse if I hit the road. For weeks after that, though, I had walked around the house bursting into frequent throaty, heartfelt renditions of "We Shall Overcome."

At one point before leaving Kansas, I had also announced to my parents that I was a pacifist and ready to lie down in front of tanks to stop the war in Vietnam.

"Did you know," I accused, "that Vietnam has claimed thirty-three thousand and six hundred fifty lives? That's more deaths than your war in Korea, Dad!"

"I don't mind if you're a pacifist," Mom told me. "Just be a cheerful pacifist, that's all I ask. Nobody likes a whiner. And for God's sake sing something else. Even Pete Seeger must get tired of that song."

Surprisingly, Dad had come to my defense. "I don't blame Holly for not supporting the war," he said. "There's no justification for it. What are we going to accomplish besides killing a lot of people and dropping a lot of expensive bombs?"

"So why don't you protest, Dad?" I'd asked. "It would mean a lot more if you stood up against the war than a million college students."

Dad had considered me for a moment, his face impassive,

masked. "It's my duty to serve," he said. "I'm not going to tell the men I teach, men who are trying to do their best by this country, that I think what they're doing is wrong."

Now Dad was coming back toward the car. Sadly, there were no hippies in the house. "Somebody must've abandoned that vehicle," he announced. "Everything's fine inside. You can unpack the car, kids."

We saluted him, because it always made him so mad, and went inside.

The movers had delivered our furniture and boxes. The dining room chairs were lined along the walls as if for a dance in a church basement. The couch floated in the middle of the living room, and the tables and lamps stood about as randomly as if someone had dropped them from the sky. It had snowed inside the family room through holes in the farmhouse walls, and the boxes and furniture were powdered white. Soft drifts of snow edged the walls like rolled-up bedsheets.

"I guess one thing we need to do is get that snow out of the house," Mom said, then closed the family room door so she wouldn't have to think about that yet.

That night, we made dinner by opening cans from the dozens of boxes we'd carried in from the car. "Isn't it great that we have something to eat right here on hand?" asked Dad, a fervent aficionado of Dinty Moore's canned beef stew. "We don't have to go anywhere! Think of the money we're saving. Why, it wouldn't even matter if this little snow turned into a blizzard. We'd be fine here for days. Maybe weeks."

"Months," Mom said, spooning a jar of applesauce into little Philip.

We were just finishing our various cans of dinner when the poodle started barking in a newly deranged way. We all got up and ran into the front hall. Beau was poised at the bottom of the staircase, trembling, his head cocked at a lump moving under the stair runner. A small trail of pee showed which way he'd run into the hall.

Donald went over and slapped his hand on the bottom step. The poodle started barking again as the lump under the rug moved faster.

"Rats! My God!" Mom moaned. She fled back to the kitchen and scooped up Philip while Dad, Donald, and I tried to catch the rat in a saucepan. This was unsuccessful. The animal eluded us by moving under the stair runner all the way downstairs, where it disappeared into a hole in the wall.

As Mom mopped up after the poodle, we heard Samantha meowing. Siamese cats have peculiar cries; if you didn't know what it was, you might think someone was strangling a baby while playing a Jew's harp. We traced this noise to the wall where the rat had disappeared. Somehow, Samantha had maneuvered her way into the tiny hole in the horsehair plaster to chase after the rat. Now she was stuck.

"We'll have to break down the wall," Dad said.

"Over my dead body," Mom said. "That cat managed to get in there. She'll just have to get out on her own. At least with the cat in there, the rat won't come back out." She turned a cold shoulder on the cat's pitiful noises. "We'll buy rat poison in the morning," she added. Mom put Philip to bed upstairs, then said she was going to take a nap on the couch.

"You kids go help your mother while I unpack the kitchen," Dad commanded.

"How can we help her?" Donald asked. "She's sleeping."

"I don't care," Dad said. "Just find something useful to do."

Dad started unpacking the kitchen. Donald fed cardboard boxes into the fireplace, where Dad had built a fire to take the chill out of the downstairs rooms. The upstairs was even colder, I realized, as I felt my way along the hallway, trying light switches that didn't work. When I discovered that the tiny box designated to be my bedroom had no heat other than the pale warmth rising from the kitchen through a metal grate in the floor, I began calculating how long it would take me to hitchhike back to Kansas.

I noticed a transom over the door, a small, multipaned window. Was I supposed to open it to let in more heat? I squinted up at the odd little window, puzzling over something dark hanging from its sill. At last, still mystified, I reached up and poked at the black shape. It swooped toward me and flew into my bedroom, where it darted into every corner before finding the doorway and zooming out again.

I screamed and ran downstairs. "Dad, Dad! There's a bat flying around upstairs!"

He picked up the kitchen broom and buckled on one of my mother's riding helmets, then galloped upstairs like Don Quixote.

When this drama had subsided, I went back to unpacking my bedroom, fantasizing about hitchhiking to San Francisco. After a while, my fingers were numb from the cold. I went back downstairs to see if there was anything to eat besides canned goods.

Dad was back at his post in the kitchen, marooned in a sea

of opened boxes. "There's no ice cream!" I accused him, flinging the freezer open twice to be sure.

"Of course there's no ice cream," Dad said. "We just got here. Nobody's been to the commissary yet. Open a can of beef stew if you're still hungry."

"I don't want beef stew!" I wailed. "And there probably isn't any commissary! We'll probably have to drive five thousand miles for a *Coke*!"

Donald showed up just then. He looked as nervous as the poodle, but at least he wasn't dribbling pee on the floor. "I think there's a problem with the fire," he said.

Dad paused in his unpacking. "What kind of problem?"

"I think it's too big," Donald said.

In the living room, smoke was pouring out of the fireplace. Mom was awake now, sitting up and coughing on the couch. "Guess I'd better go upstairs and get the baby," she said, and took the stairs two at a time.

"What the hell did you do now, Donald?" Dad yelled.

"I was helping! I was breaking down boxes!" Donald yelled back. "It was just really hard to get the refrigerator box to fit in the fireplace!"

"Jesus Christ," Dad said, stunned by the sheer size of the problem crackling in front of us. The smoke was starting to curl through the house. Meanwhile, it was ten degrees outside and still snowing. "Goddamn it," he said. "I think the chimney's on fire. Let's hope we don't lose the roof. You kids get out of here while I call the fire department."

We couldn't find the cat. Mom, my brothers, and I sat in the car with the whimpering poodle while firemen scrambled around on our icy roof to put out the fire. Embers were shooting out of the chimney into the night sky like fireworks.

Other cars started arriving. Vehicles filled with families pulled into our yard or parked on the frozen field across the street. People climbed out of them and stood about in small groups, faces lit by the flames.

"I bet this is what Woodstock was like," I told Mom, who sat in the front seat with Philip on her lap. She kept the engine running to keep us warm despite Dad's strict orders not to waste gas.

"Except that these people are wearing jackets instead of dancing around naked," she said. "Thank God."

Dad stood around outside, too, talking and joking with the firemen as if he were hosting a party. We watched him gesture at the fire trucks and flames as if he'd meant for all of this to happen.

Luckily, the roof was slate and the fire trucks had arrived in time to hose down the clapboards. A fireman tapped on Mom's window after a little while. "Should be fine to go back inside soon," he said.

"Who are all these people?" Mom asked.

The fireman shrugged and scratched his smudged nose beneath the big yellow hat. "Volunteers. They all heard the sirens."

"They aren't all firemen," Mom pointed out. "A lot of people are just standing around and watching."

"Oh, them others, you mean." The fireman grinned. "Some people just like a good fire," he said. "The Papas had one every year about this time up here at the farm with that old chimney. It's a town tradition. You new people are just keeping it going."

"I'm so glad to oblige," Mom said, and rolled up her window.

"Who were the Papas?" I asked eagerly, thinking of the Mamas and the Papas.

"I think he was saying *Paupers,*" Mom said. "That's how they talk in Massachusetts."

"What are paupers?" Donald asked.

"Poor people," Mom said. "Poor people just like us."

~

We were far from poor. Dad, always cautious, had crafted a thoroughly detailed scheme for starting his gerbil farm while finishing up his twenty years in the Navy. He commuted back and forth those first two years between Massachusetts and Long Island, where he lived in officers' quarters at the Merchant Marine Academy. His plan was to retire with the rank of commander and a reasonable Navy pension while he grew enough gerbils to ensure our financial health. To do this, he'd found a fifteen-room farmhouse on ninety acres of land that we could afford on his salary simply because it was buried in the Brookfields, the forgotten agricultural heart of Massachusetts between Boston and the Berkshires.

Nonetheless, technically we really had bought the poor farm. Our house, depending on whom you asked around West Brookfield, was known as "the old Blair Farm," "the town farm," or the "almshouse." In the years before Social Security, paupers were sent to live in state-subsidized farms managed by wardens or poor masters. They worked the land, living off the food they grew and the cows they milked.

"The transom over your window was probably put there so the warden could tell when a pauper died in his sleep," Dad teased me.

They probably died of cold, I thought, tossing and turning and shivering in my bed during those first drafty weeks in West Brookfield. Who, I wondered, had been desperate enough to live in this creaky old house before we did? Who had slept in my teeny box of a bat-friendly room, folding her few clothes into its odd built-in cupboards? And was she as miserable as I was?

For I was miserable, more miserable than I'd ever been in my life. I missed my sister but couldn't talk about her because it made Mom leave the room and Dad grind his teeth. I missed our horses, but Ladybug and Robin wouldn't arrive until spring. And most of all, I hated this farm, with its stained carpeting, peeling layers of wallpaper, noisy radiators, dribbling shower, and fields full of nothing but snow, snow, snow. Why had Dad moved us here? Gerbils had proved to be perfectly happy in basements and garages! We could have kept our horses in a stable, where there were other people to ride with! At the very least, we could have moved to a town within forty miles of a movie theater!

I spent that first chilly week on the poor farm giving my parents the silent treatment.

"A vacation for our ears," Dad pronounced, while Mom communicated her requests for help with household chores through notes taped onto the bathroom mirror.

In my bedroom, I tried on clothes and discarded them, or

read books I'd already read. At one point, I was bored enough to iron my own hair, an idea I'd read about in *Seventeen* magazine. I managed to raise long, red, angry blisters across my forehead when I pressed the iron too close to my scalp in an attempt to flatten my wavy bangs, prompting Donald to dub me "Little Miss Frankenstein."

Mom yelled at me for branding my own forehead. I stormed outside and stomped across the thick icy crust over the snow. It was a dramatic escape toward the woods behind our house, like a settler fleeing the murderous savages. Unfortunately, the icy crust layered over the snow wasn't thick enough to hold my weight, so my feet punched through the ice again and again until welts rose on my ankles to match the ones on my forehead.

After a few dozen tortured steps, I threw myself down onto the snow, howling at the gray sky until I realized that Mom, Donald, and little Phil were all watching me from the kitchen window. Mom waved.

A minute later, she opened the back door. "Why don't you come inside?" she called. "It's too cold to be lying around in that snow."

"How could you let Dad bring us here?" I screamed at her. "What am I supposed to *do*?"

Mom gestured at the cup in her hand. "The only thing you need to do today is come inside and have some hot chocolate," she said.

Chapter Eleven

Nobody's Business but Ours

Grandfather and Philip in the garden

CREDIT: THE HOLLY ROBINSON COLLECTION

Once the gerbils entered our lives,

Mom and Dad lived according to this solid-gold credo: "What we do is nobody's business."

Now that we were in Massachusetts, Dad brought us a few steps closer to the cliff edge of deepest anonymity. He'd chosen to buy the poor farm in West Brookfield not just because it was affordable and within a day's drive of an airport but also because it was on the way to nowhere. After his retirement from the Navy in two years, there would be no military brass to rip the bars off his uniform if his secret passion for the pocket kangaroo was unveiled. In the meantime, he wanted to ensure that his fellow officers at the Merchant Marine Academy remained in the dark about how the heck he spent his free time.

Dad was also worried about the long-term repercussions of raising gerbils on a large scale. Leftist politics were seeping into everything from women in the workplace to U.S. involvement abroad. That included increasingly vocal animal rights activists. Dad planned to raise gerbils not as pets, but to sell to researchers engaged in scientific studies; the more under the radar he could keep us, the better.

To this end, my father now devised an ingenious cover-up to disguise his intent: he made the gerbil farm look like a horse farm. In historical papers held at the town library describing the history of our property, the "almshouse" was "sold to William Shaw, later sold to Mark V. Crockett. Mr. Crockett sold the fields and wooded land to the Wildlife Preserve of Mass. And the remainder to Tumblebrook Farm, a riding stable operated by D. G. Robinson."

Of course, establishing a convincing front meant bringing the horses from Kansas to Massachusetts and building a barn for them, a plan that Mom and I immediately took to heart. None of us knew a thing about barn raising, but luckily we had reinforcements. My mother's parents, Maybelle and Everett Keach, came to live with us shortly after New Year's, dragging a rickety trailer full of their belongings all the way from Virginia. The trailer came unhitched from the car on its last gasp up Long Hill Road and rolled backward into a stone wall, but we managed to retrieve most of their belongings—a few bits of antique pine furniture, pots and pans, Grandfather's gardening tools—and installed our grandparents in the small in-law apartment upstairs.

My grandparents were no strangers to hard work. Maybelle had been born in England and arrived in Boston by ship with her father, recruited by the New England mills as an expert wool sorter, and her mother, a girl with a streak of wildness that led her to abandon her family at age thirty-five for an eighteen-year-old lover. Grandmother was fifteen years old at the time of her mother's defection. The oldest of five children, she was luckier than her siblings: her own grandmother, who had also divorced her first husband, had remarried a British sergeant major named Peter Pickles, so she was in a good position to take young Maybelle in hand.

While my grandmother's two younger sisters toiled away at menial jobs and her two younger brothers labored in factories from an early age, Grandmother was able to finish high school, take piano lessons, learn to pour a proper tea, and wear gloves and a hat to the Methodist church. She turned into a steely sort of woman determined to be nothing like her own wandering mother, but known far and wide for her impeccable housekeeping, charitable acts, good manners, and tidy children.

Her only weakness was Grandfather, whom she met at age sixteen and fell for like a sack of sugar knocked off a table by a baseball bat. As a young man, my grandfather, Everett, was a natty dresser who talked Grandmother into taking off the woolen bloomers she wore under her dress and stashing them under the bushes before joining him on the back of his motorcycle for furiously fast rides. She married him at age seventeen and had three children by the time she was twenty-one years old.

It was difficult for me to imagine the ardor of this courtship. By the time Grandfather moved in with us, he was a balding, terse, bespectacled man in a flannel shirt who was never without a pipe and a Dixie cup of liquid courage at his elbow. He wore broad-brimmed hats, told raunchy jokes, read three mystery novels a week, and rode low in the seat of his old car at speeds that made you wonder why he didn't just walk. He had his own inexplicable passion for Native Americans, which meant that he was always ferreting around for arrowheads and had a collection of Indian headdresses hanging in the basement that scared the bejesus out of you whenever you rounded the corner into his basement workshop.

But Grandfather was handy with a toolbox, no matter how many bottles of homemade wine or cheap whiskey he kept stashed around the basement. When my father discovered an abandoned dairy barn on the 350 acres of land across the street that had originally belonged to the poor farm and was now conservation land, he petitioned the state for permission to disassemble the building. Dad and Grandfather constructed a wooden cart and attached it to a wheezing red tractor purchased from a neighboring farm. We used this clanking Dr. Seuss contraption to haul enormous, knotholed planks of ancient lumber and anything else we could salvage from the original pole barn to our property: hinges, nails and screws, and even a few dented buckets.

With the recycled lumber, we had enough to build a stable behind the house with stalls for a dozen horses; Dad did this with the idea that we would take in boarders. "If you and your mother are going to keep horses, we might as well let other people pay for the grain," he said.

In addition to the wood, the original dairy barn also had milking stanchions and all sorts of other peculiar, torturous-looking metal odds and ends, which Grandfather cut and welded to make hay bins, bars for the stalls, and gates for the pastures.

The horses arrived that spring, when lush beds of wild daffodils sprang out of the ground and the magnolia tree outside our kitchen window bloomed with flowers as pink and delicate as Grandmother's English teacups. As I unloaded Ladybug from the horse trailer and threw my arms around her neck, it suddenly seemed possible to me that I might survive on the farm after all.

Donald and I explored the trails and logging roads behind the house all spring, with me on horseback and Donald zipping around on an old dirt bike he'd found abandoned somewhere on Long Hill Road and coaxed back to life. I'd trot Ladybug along the trails through the dappled light of the huge trees bowed over the cart roads, while in the pasture next to me Donald flew over dirt moguls and sometimes was separated from his bike in midair. Neither of us would admit it, but Donald and I were glad for each other's company.

By May, Donald and Dad were making monthly pilgrimages to Victor Schwentker's house in Brant Lake, renting a twenty-four-foot U-Haul truck to ferry back everything necessary for a gerbil colony: cages and metal shelves, water bottles and feeding hoppers, filing cabinets and desks, and crates of gerbils. We wheeled the crates into the basement through the door beneath the sundeck and stacked the new gerbils on shelves next to the glass jars that Grandmother used for preserving fruit and vegetables.

With our horses grazing in the field beside the house, probably no one passing by would ever suspect—well, really, who would?—that in the basement of the old poor farm we were seeding a new crop of gerbils.

MY PARENTS chose the Lake Wickaboag Boat Club as their point of entry into West Brookfield social life. Boats, water, and cocktail parties: the Boat Club was the one place where they felt they might fit in.

If you saw West Brookfield from an airplane, Lake Wickaboag would sit at its center like a green eye with marshy lashes. Some townspeople belonged to the Boat Club—the families with any money, that is—but most members were summer families from Connecticut, New York, New Jersey, and Pennsylvania who came to West Brookfield every summer to vacation in lakeside camps that had been in their families for generations.

The Lake Wickaboag Boat Club was, despite its grand name, a mushroom of a place, a tiny pseudo log cabin on a weedy beach. Naturally, Dad revealed nothing about the true nature of his farm to the Boat Club members; they were under the impression that he was a military bigwig who had chosen to have a hobby farm. The members of the Boat Club were so besotted with the idea of having a real live Navy commander in their midst that they invited Dad to don his Navy uniform and ride in the lead boat that summer during the Memorial Day parade. Dad enjoyed every minute of it, perfecting what Mom called "your Royal Navy wave to the landlubbers" from the bow of the boat. Despite this overwhelming welcome, my parents didn't stay members for long.

"Those people are all so boring," Mom said with a sniff. "All very provincial. And your father never was much of a dancer."

The kids in town used to spy on the adult parties at the Boat Club, and they didn't look boring to us. One Saturday night, the skinny woman I babysat for, the mother of three boys under the age of four, climbed onto the bar and shimmied along the tops of the exposed beams in the ceiling like a miniskirted serpent. Another man perfected a trick of his own, removing the bras of various women by pulling them out of the armholes of their sleeveless dresses like a Hindu snake charmer urging cobras out of baskets.

There was rampant swapping among the various couples on the lake, too. So many marriages went down in flames that on the sign on Route 9 that said "Welcome to West Brookfield," someone scrawled out the town's name that summer and substituted it with "Peyton Place."

~

As before, Donald and I were operating under stern orders not to speak of the gerbils outside the family. This was a needless command. We were savvy enough to know that we weren't going to break into any school cliques with gerbils as our calling cards.

Donald and I started school midyear. He was in sixth grade at the local elementary school and had little trouble adjusting. Donald was savvier than his eleven-year-old peers, faster on his bicycle, and an ace shot with his BB gun. He'd seen enough Army drills in Kansas to understand the basic principles of attack and defend.

My brother established his position high on the West Brookfield food chain early on thanks to a single incident: when one of the tough kids in town stole his bike, Donald said, "You'd better give that back or I'll shoot you in the leg." When the boy refused, Donald got his BB gun and shot that kid right in the leg.

"That'll teach them to mess with you," Mom said.

Things didn't go as smoothly for me. I was in ninth grade at Quaboag Regional High School, which served the mill towns of Warren and West Warren in addition to West Brookfield. The school lived up to its nickname of "Little Poland": the bus driver played polkas on the radio, Polish was spoken in the halls, and Polish food was served in the cafeteria.

Compared to my high school at Fort Leavenworth, with its straight lines, quiet classrooms, and routine inspections, anarchy ruled at Quaboag in the early 1970s. The lockers, a complicated maze at one end of the cafeteria, were rich with the heady aromas of pot and booze, and there were daily brawls with creative weaponry, like the pointy ends of shop compasses. With my bookish tendencies and absurd accent—Tidewater Virginia overlaid with Kansas twang—I fit into this school like a gerbil among a pack of coyotes.

Rumor had it at Quaboag that my parents were rich, which we were, in relative terms, living as we did in that big house on top of Long Hill Road. Even if the house was falling down around our ears, we had fifteen rooms all to ourselves. More than one kid came up to ask me how we'd gotten our money. "Oh, you know. My dad's military," I'd answer vaguely.

Rumor had it that my mysterious father was either CIA or a tax-dodging millionaire, and my new clothes (despite being from Sears) and horses must mean that I was an heiress. Even if I had not been forbidden from telling the truth, I knew it would do nothing to help my reputation to admit that my father's aspiration in life was to be a gerbil farmer.

By the boys at Quaboag, I was warmly welcomed, flirted with, teased, and fought over. Chalk that up to novelty and to the breasts that had accompanied me all the way from Kansas. However, it is a given in high school that if the boys like you too much, the girls won't like you at all.

My first month at Quaboag, three of the girls made it clear that I was not welcome. The girls had lovely names, the hopeful romantic imaginings of mothers raised on a steady diet of TV soap operas: Clarissa, Donna, and Sheri. But they were not lovely girls. Clarissa had biceps the circumference of my waist. Donna wore men's blue work trousers and work boots. Sheri had sharp hatchet features and the unblinking, mesmerizing green eyes of a serial killer.

My harpies were assigned to the standard, twiddle-your-thumbs vocational classes, which served as a holding pen for teenagers too young to drop out and work at the local lace factory. This meant that I was safe while tucked inside my college-prep classes. Eventually, however, I'd have to join the bodies swimming upstream to the gym or the lockers and the girls would track me down.

Shortly after I started freshman year at the high school that January, the girls began their torment with a whispering campaign. They'd hound me in the hallways and follow so close behind me that I could feel their hot cigarette breath on my neck as I race-walked down the hallways to avoid them.

"Holly Robinson sucks," they whispered.

"Holly Robinson sucks donkey dick," they whispered.

"Holly Robinson could suck the bumper off a car," they said.

I began inventing new ways to get from one class to the other, sliding through the darkened theater to cut between hallways or making excuses to stop by the main office until, seconds before the bell rang, I could make a dash for safety. Once I made the mistake of trying to hide in one of the bathrooms. Clarissa, Donna, and Sheri were seated on the gray horseshoe-shaped sink, having lunch and smoking a joint, when I came bursting through the door.

Clarissa slipped between me and the bathroom door before I could get out. "Do you know how bad you suck?" she asked, hooking her thumbs into the waistband of her hip-hugger jeans. This had the unfortunate effect of distending her belly even more over the jeans, and it suddenly dawned on me that she was pregnant. My immediate thought was that at least I couldn't have more than eight more months of this torture.

"Why do you hate me so much?" I asked. "I haven't done anything."

"We don't hate you," Sheri said, stepping up alongside Clarissa, a carton of milk from the lunchroom in her hand. "We just hate the way you *look*. It *offends* us." She tipped the carton of milk upside down over my head and spilled the contents into my hair. "There. Now *that's* a big fucking improvement."

The three of them howled as I fled the bathroom, wiping the milk from my face.

That afternoon, as I was pulling books out of my locker as fast as I could to make the bus, Clarissa sneaked up to pin me against the locker. "Hit me, bitch!" she screamed. "Hit me so that I can nail you good in self-defense!"

Her blue eyes were narrowed by pot and she stank of beer. She was waving a shop compass in one hand, the metal point gleaming like a switchblade. A crowd gathered around us and started the usual chanting.

"Fight, fight, fight!"

I took a deep breath. "I can't do that," I said. "I'm a pacifist."

"Figures you'd suck pacifiers, too," howled Donna, who

stood behind Clarissa with her work boots planted wide as the sky.

"No," I said. "I'm a pacifist. That means that I'm morally opposed to violence. If you hit me, I still can't hit you back." Maybe they would knock me out, I thought. Then I could just go to sleep and not wake up.

"God, you are such a fucking weirdo loser," Clarissa said, and turned away to repeat my manifesto to her friends. The three of them doubled over and laughed like hyenas, giving me the chance to slip away.

~

DAD needn't have worried about anyone making a fuss about the gerbils. In West Brookfield there were three types of people: those who worked locally and had always lived in West Brookfield, occupying the modest capes and ranch houses on the newer streets in town; the few newcomers who worked in Worcester or Springfield and were starting to buy up the huge antique Colonials around the common; and the families of children like Donna, Clarissa and Sheri, who rented the sagging bungalows and apartments in the two-story buildings along the railroad tracks bordering the outskirts of West Brookfield like a tattered hem.

Beyond those railroad tracks, Long Hill Road was the lawless frontier. In fact, among our Long Hill neighbors, we stood out as one of the more normal families.

Just down the street in a small shack lived a family with so many members of different sizes that we couldn't keep track of how they were related. The one thing they all had in common besides missing teeth was their white-blond hair and pink-rimmed eyes, leading Mom to dub them "the Albinos."

The Albinos wrapped their house in plastic. Not just their windows but their entire house was annually shrink-wrapped to keep out the cold. The plastic usually started to rip in places within a month of being tacked onto the house, so it sounded like applause whenever a good breeze came up.

In the winter, the Albino children wore plastic bread bags wrapped around their feet instead of boots, so you could always hear them coming and going. Their cars were wrapped, too: plastic on the windows, and duct tape on the rusted bumpers and wheel wells so that they'd pass inspection. You always knew that the Albinos were driving by when you heard the whistle and whip of those streamers trailing behind their cars.

At the bottom of Long Hill Road, next to the railroad tracks, lived Whitey, a gold-toothed motorcyclist who built his own race cars in his yard and gave Donald essential tips on beating the cops at their own game. With Whitey as his mentor, Donald knew every speed trap by the age of fourteen and even managed to hoist the police chief's canoe off the town beach and bring it up to the house. Later, when Donald got his driver's license, Whitey taught him how to cut a hole in the floor of your car so that you could just push the empty beer cans through it if the cops happened to give chase on an unlucky Saturday night.

There was a furniture factory on Long Hill Road, too, run by Seventh Day Adventists who wore black polyester trousers no matter how hot it was, with button-down shirts and shiny black shoes. On quiet days, you could almost dance to the popping rhythm of the staple guns and the hum of buzz saws as the Adventists produced conveyor belts of plywood-backed bookcases and bureaus in the name of God.

Among our most immediate neighbors, probably the most integrated into society was the owner of the hearse parked in our driveway that first night. His name was Dennis Clark, and he was an artist and a musician who taught at another area high school. The hearse had been in our driveway because it had broken down there while he helped the former occupants move out. Dennis sold it shortly afterward because, as handy as that car might be for moving musical instruments, the cops always stopped him in it. "I just don't understand why," he told us. "It's almost like they want to run me out of town."

Dennis lived with his wife and two children in a squat white cape made decorous by hex signs. In addition to painting hex signs and hearses in his spare time, he had crafted a special coffin-shaped cart for his own father. As the weather warmed up, he would set his aged pops in the coffin cart and pull it out to the sunny corner of the yard overlooking the road. The frail old man looked as though he might topple into the path of your oncoming car as he lifted a scrawny arm to wave at you passing by.

"At least if the old man gets run over, they can roll him right on over to the cemetery in that thing," Mom said.

The first time I visited the Clarks was to sell magazines, a fund-raiser for the high school. I walked down the street one Saturday, waved at the old man on the lawn, and knocked on the door. It opened almost immediately. Facing me in the doorway wasn't Dennis Clark or his wife, though, but a tall brown-and-white goat with the long silky ears of a basset hound. For an instant I thought the goat must have turned the knob. Then Dennis popped his head around the corner, a skinny, amiable man with big glasses and a beard like a paintbrush.

"Come in, come in!" he insisted. "I was just practicing my mandolin." He strummed a chord to demonstrate, which made the goat trot back outside through the double doors leading out to the yard, leaving a trail of raisin-sized dung pellets along the dining room floor.

As I stared, Dennis laughed. "Don't worry about the goats. Those are Nubians. They're from Africa and they're very sweet pets. It's like having big poodles around, only more useful. They'll clear out your yard, even the poison ivy. So, to what do I owe the pleasure of your esteemed company?"

"I'm selling magazines to raise money for the high school," I said.

"Always a good cause, always," Dennis murmured, but made no move to extract his checkbook. He just stood there grinning, as if waiting for me to sing a birthday telegram.

"Thank you for seeing me," I said after a moment, and started to turn away.

"Wait, wait!" he protested. "We're neighbors! We should take this opportunity to get to know each other!" He went to the kitchen and returned with a glass of apple cider. "Have a cooling refreshment, at least. Now tell me. How are you settling in?"

"Fine."

"Are you enjoying school here?" He narrowed his eyes, as if he could see right through my skin to my bruised heart.

"It's okay. It's school," I said.

This seemed to please him. "That's the spirit," he said.

"You'll find your kin, don't worry. It just takes time. It's not easy being new."

"No," I agreed.

"So what are your parents going to do with that big farm?" he asked.

I nearly choked on the cider. Nobody had ever asked me so directly before. "We have horses," I hedged.

"Oh! Horses, yes, they're always fun," Dennis said dismissively. "But isn't your father going to do something, well, a little more *interesting*?"

"I'm not sure what you mean," I said.

Dennis grinned. "That house has always had interesting people in it, you know. In fact, this whole *street*." He waved his hand, including all of Long Hill Road in that single sweeping gesture. "For instance, there was a multiracial family in my house before I bought it." Dennis lowered his voice as if the Klan might be lurking around the corner. "They were members of those Catholic Communists, the Dorothy Day movement. The commune's right down the road in Brookfield. Everyone on this road was supporting Abbie Hoffman, in fact. I'm sure you've heard of him."

I nodded.

Again Dennis beamed. "Well, the people in this neighborhood were all Catholic radicals. They took a vow of poverty but didn't believe in birth control, so you can imagine the disaster *that* was."

I thought of the Albinos and nodded again.

Dennis went on to talk about the history of the Native Americans on Long Hill Road and the artifacts taken from the hill to a Springfield museum. On our land, he said, there was a maize grinding stone the size of a small room. The original schoolhouse in West Brookfield had once been on poor-farm land, too, until it was rolled down the hill by oxen on logs in 1917.

"During the 1920s, the government raised bison on poor-farm land," he added. "That was part of the movement to repopulate the buffalo herds in America." He cocked his head at me. "Your father's not going to raise buffalo, by any chance?"

I laughed. Not because it was such a strange suggestion, but because it would have been such a relief to tell people that we were doing something as normal as raising a few hundred head of bison.

Dennis nodded. "I'm just yanking your chain, man. I know what your dad's up to."

I was more shocked by this than by the goat in the dining room. "You do?"

"Oh, sure. Your dad told me all about his new venture. And I don't mind it a bit. I doubt anybody up here on Long Hill Road would protest a gerbil farm. You don't have to worry. You know what I did before moving out here?"

I shook my head.

"I was a laboratory animal caretaker!" Dennis said, slapping one blue-jeaned thigh. "Man, now what kind of cosmic joke is that?" He took my empty glass, walked it over to the kitchen, and rinsed it out in the sink as he told me how laboratory animals had put him through art school.

"I was an animal caretaker at Brown University when I was at Rhode Island School of Design," Dennis said. "I took care of all sorts of exotic animals: bush babies, lemurs, cobras, rattlesnakes, spiders."

"You did?" I was rooted to the spot, fascinated, and feeling something I hadn't felt in a long time: accepted.

Dennis nodded. "The oddest animal was a spinny mouse. They do backflips to scare their enemies. I'd hear them spinning in their cages all day long, *ba-doop, ba-doop, ba-doop*."

His favorite lab animals, though, were the lemurs. "They have the most human-like skin," Dennis explained. "Almost human ears. They're from Madagascar. I used to take live mice in to feed them. I'd toss the mice into the cages, and the lemurs caught them with their hands like baseball players catching fly balls. Then they'd pop them right into their mouths and chew those mice up like popcorn!"

As Dennis walked me to the door, he clapped a hand on my shoulder. "You just tell your dad not to worry about the neighbors, okay? We're cool. You are, too. You just don't know it yet."

Chapter Twelve

Do It Yourself or Die Trying

From THE USE OF GERBILS IN SCIENCE EDUCATION

CREDIT: D. G. ROBINSON JR.

On the farm, there were more chores to do than hours in a day. As Mom put it, "This house has been really abused. There are lots of loose things about it." Like the settlers who had made similarly arduous journeys to stake a claim, we used hard work as a salve for grief and loss.

While Dad spent weekdays in New York, teaching at the Merchant Marine Academy, the rest of us peeled off old wallpaper, patched and painted walls, yanked up stained carpeting, and scraped layers of yellow enamel off the stair railings. We brightened the dark kitchen paneling with white paint and hung wallpaper in places where the house would have fallen apart without that extra gluey layer holding it together.

One Friday, I came home from school and interrupted Mom in the middle of taking down an entire wall with a crowbar. "I've always wanted to do this," she declared, wiping plaster dust off her cheek. "There's nothing like a little demolition to relieve stress."

"What are you so worried about, Mom?" I asked.

She glanced at the clock. "Your father's due back from

New York any minute, and you know he'll find something to criticize."

Mom put down the crowbar, went into the kitchen and poured herself a glass of water. She took two Alka-Seltzer tablets out of her jeans pocket and dropped them into the glass. "Plop plop, fizz fizz," she said with a smile that didn't reach her eyes, and gulped down the contents of the glass just as we heard Dad's car pull into the driveway.

"Holly! Donald! Where are you?" Dad shouted as he came up the basement stairs, running as usual.

"Welcome home, dear," Mom said as Dad threw open the door and heaved his duffel bag full of the week's laundry off his shoulder and onto the floor.

Dad's smile was like Mom's: half grimace. He nodded at me and said, "Go get your brother and clean out my car. Now."

"Yes, sir." I ran down the basement stairs and found Donald in the workshop with Grandfather, gluing the spindles back into an old chair that Grandfather had found by the side of the road. "Dad's home," I said.

"O Captain! my Captain!" Grandfather said.

"We have to clean out the car," I said. "Right now, or he'll be mad. You know how he is."

"Why do *we* have to do it every Friday? It's *his* mess," Donald grumbled, but he followed me out to the driveway.

By the time we came back inside, Dad had changed out of his Navy uniform and was squinting at the new blue-and-white kitchen wallpaper that Mom and Grandfather had put up that week, a tumbler of scotch in one hand. "Looks about an eighth of an inch off to me," he pronounced. "That's a shame, considering what wallpaper costs a roll. I hope you got it on sale."

Grandmother came downstairs to join us in the kitchen, a flowered apron tied around her tweed skirt. "I baked you an apple pie, Robbie," she said.

"Thank you, Mother, but there was really no need. We eat too many sweets," Dad said, still eyeing the wallpaper. "How much electricity do you suppose that old oven of yours uses?"

"Come look, Dad," I said, leading him over to the kitchen window overlooking the back garden and the pastures beyond. "Donald and I cleared a lot of rocks out of the pasture. We filled in some of the woodchuck holes, too."

"Your grandfather mowed the grass again, I see," Dad said. "I never did care too much for manicured lawns. Mowers use an awful lot of gas, you know."

Grandfather had come up from the basement by now and was standing with his arms folded across his chest. The last of the sunset glinted against his glasses so that I couldn't read his expression. "Might as well let the grass grow up around you, then, and live in a jungle," he said. "You'd save a hell of a lot of pennies that way." He turned on his heel and went upstairs.

"Well, I'll leave you all to enjoy your dinner," Grandmother said. She set her pie down on the counter before following Grandfather up to their apartment.

"Now look what you've done," Mom said.

"What? What did I do?" Dad asked. "Can't a man express an honest opinion around here without everyone taking it so personally? After all, I've bent over backward to give your parents a place to live. I should have some say in things."

"Hitler would have more tact," Mom said.

Dad may have given my grandparents a home, but they worked hard to earn it. The very next day, for instance, my father returned from taking the trash to the dump and called Grandfather outside to see what he'd brought home. Donald and I followed Grandfather out to the driveway, where the back of Dad's red Ford station wagon was crammed with dirty flat sticks he'd collected at the dump.

"What is that stuff?" I asked Dad. "Kindling?"

He shook his head. "If you just wire these together, Dad," he told Grandfather, "I bet we can make a snow fence all along the road."

"Damn fool," Grandfather muttered behind me. "Spindly little things will fall down in the first storm."

Somehow, though, Grandfather managed to build a fence from those discarded slats of wood, and it never did fall down.

~

SHORTLY after we moved to Massachusetts, Dad gave us a lecture on keeping the lights off and the heat down. "Now that the military's not paying our utility bills, it's important to remember that frugal is our middle name," he said as he showed us how to make Christmas ornaments out of scraps of old wallpaper that we'd peeled off the kitchen and hallway walls.

As the cold set in, Dad made a habit of feeling the pipes when he got home on Fridays to make sure that nobody had turned up the heat; luckily, Mom knew enough to turn the heat down on Friday mornings so that the pipes would cool in time.

That first Christmas, Dad said there was no money for a Christmas tree, so Donald and I hiked out to the woods behind the house, cut down a tree, and dragged it home, a practice we would repeat every year after that. Grandfather nailed together bits of scrap wood and painted them to make Christmas trees for either side of our front door. He also fashioned a candelabra out of old spools of thread and spray-painted it black so that we could use it as a centerpiece during Christmas dinner.

Grandmother did her part, too. She hand-quilted garlands of candy canes, angels, and soldiers to wrap around the front staircase, and crocheted red and green holiday covers for the extra rolls of toilet paper sitting on top of the toilet tank. The next fall, she started making apple-head dolls to sell at church fairs, using empty Clorox bottles for the bodies and pinching the dried-up apples into eerie little grimacing gremlin faces. I felt sorry for any kid whose mother came home with one of *those,* despite the hours Grandmother spent stitching dresses and aprons and hats for her apple-headed horrors.

Where I was concerned, Dad was a stop-spending vigilante. I had already cost him more money than any of my siblings because of my teeth. Those first few weeks after my riding accident in Kansas, I'd had to keep my lips pressed shut to hide my toothless gums while they healed. An Army dentist had then crafted a temporary bridge attached to a plastic roof plate. This contraption was held in place by a few strategic wires that fit into the cracks between my remaining front teeth.

The only good thing about the accident, other than losing my snaggletooth, was that I now had a surefire way to unnerve my father. He had a much softer stomach than Mom, who could pluck ticks the size of grapes off the dogs with her bare hands and inject medicine into a horse with a needle the size of a milk shake straw. Anytime Dad lectured or scolded, I'd use my tongue to flip the bridge down, revealing the gap where my front teeth had been. At the sight of my bright pink gums, he'd blanch and turn away.

"Jesus Christ, Holly," he'd mutter. "Don't do that to me."

That first year in Massachusetts, I was outfitted with a permanent bridge—a nifty, wire-free cosmetic design not covered by military health insurance. I could no longer flip my front teeth at Dad because they were permanently anchored into place by crowns on teeth that hadn't been knocked out. This meant that I had a straight-toothed smile and no longer had to worry about losing my teeth at inopportune moments, as I had in Kansas, where I routinely had to dive to the bottom of the pool to retrieve them.

The down side of having such an expensive mouth was that Dad would materialize from nowhere to issue warnings anytime I ventured outside. "Your teeth, Holly!" he'd cry, trotting after me as I set off on horseback. "Watch out for your teeth! Those cost money we don't have, you know!"

He was also extremely watchful of my toilet paper consumption. Whenever I used our only bathroom upstairs, I had to turn the toilet paper roll as stealthily as possible, because if he heard me using it, Dad would come pounding up the stairs to knock on the bathroom door.

"You don't need more than three squares, Holly!" he'd yell. "Remember, more than three squares is wasted!"

Eventually, I solved this problem by buying toilet paper

with my own babysitting money, a separate stash that I kept in my bedroom and carried back and forth to silently unwrap, counting out five squares just because I could.

~

IN THE steady, dauntless way of pioneers, we slowly began to make the farm feel like home. Grandfather planted a huge garden behind the house, one-half of which was devoted to tall, brightly colored flowers—Grandmother adored gladioli, so we had more of those than anything else—while from the other half we reaped peas and beans, tomatoes and cucumbers, lettuce and squash.

After dinner each night, Grandfather patrolled his garden for weeds and evidence of rabbits or woodchucks, a pipe in his mouth. Sylvester, a Siamese cat he and my grandmother doted on like a favored son, tagged along at Grandfather's heels and rubbed up against an occasional cabbage, so cross-eyed that the rabbits could hop about anywhere they liked, unhindered by the cat's presence.

Grandfather's vegetables were so extraordinary in size and color, so unlike anything we'd ever brought home from the commissary, that they looked like the irradiated food I'd read about in science fiction novels.

"How do you get the squash to grow this big?" I asked one day as we collected gourds with the size and heft of artificial limbs.

"Oh, that's an old family secret." Grandfather filled his pipe and lit it, then leaned forward to whisper, "It's all about having enough horseshit to go around. And there's no shortage of *that* in this family."

~

SEIZED by the pioneering spirit, I decided to build a house of my own. I went to the West Brookfield Library and checked out a book called something like *How Even the Dumbest People Can Build Houses*. I drew up house plans that depended on using salvaged wood from the dairy barns across the street—there seemed to be an endless supply—and the old windows from the three-sided greenhouse that had once been attached to our farmhouse and now lay in random piles behind the duck pond near the road.

On horseback, I'd found the perfect spot for my endeavor: a small hollow overlooking a shallow green pond noisy with frogs and songbirds. "Can you help me build this?" I asked Donald one night, speaking directly to his knees and calves, since the rest of my brother's lanky body was hidden beneath the body of a rusted, ancient Triumph he'd convinced Mom to buy from Whitey.

Donald slid out from beneath the car on the little wheeled cart he'd built himself for just such a purpose and examined my plans. "A house, huh?" he asked.

For once, I'd gotten Donald's attention, a rare thing for anyone, since he generally thought most people were too stupid to live. "Just a cabin," I corrected. "A place to think."

"A place to screw your boyfriends, you mean," Donald said, but he agreed to help.

He drove me across the street in the rattling jeep, so rusted in spots now that it looked like a camouflaged Army vehicle, and we collected scraps of wood from the barn. Next, we piled on the old glass windows from the greenhouse; I planned to use these as walls so that I could see the pond from any angle, despite Donald's assertion that I'd "sizzle like a steak."

With the jeep loaded and ready, we careened down the logging trail in back of the house, spooking the horses and dropping occasional panes of glass and pieces of rotted lumber as we bounced over the rutted road. Donald drove fast enough so that low overhanging branches snapped against the hood of the jeep and broke right off.

"Might as well clear the trail while we're at it," he said when I urged him to slow down.

At the pond, we unloaded what was left of the lumber and glass, and then Donald took off, leaving me alone in the woods with the deerflies, gnats, and mosquitoes feeding on my neck and arms, and only a hammer and a box of salvaged rusty nails for tools. I'd chosen the biggest nails I could find, nails longer and fatter than pencils. In my mind, the bigger the nails, the sturdier the walls.

I devoted myself to building my house every day after school for three days, bruising my thumb with the hammer, embedding splinters in my hands, and developing a case of poison ivy that left my face swollen like a doughnut.

I quit when I had a floor and one wall. I'd succeeded in building my own window onto the pond, and every now and then I'd ride one of the horses up that rutted trail to sit there and stare through the glass at the weeds and water, swatting bugs off my neck.

~

DURING our first year in Massachusetts, Dad and Donald made about fifteen trips to Brant Lake to gather gerbils and gerbil-growing supplies. My father didn't want to waste pennies on a motel, so he did the ten-hour round trip to Brant Lake in a single day, leaving home early on Saturday and arriving in time for Mildred Schwentker to feed them sandwiches.

On the way home, if Donald begged hard enough, they'd stop at a McDonald's, sideswiping curbs with the U-Haul trailer full of rattling metal gerbil cages and shelves as Dad wheeled in and out of the parking lots. They never once ate inside a restaurant, because Dad always believed that sitting in a fast-food place defeated the true purpose of its existence. Besides, time was money.

By the time we'd accumulated a few hundred breeding pairs in our basement, Dad was ready to build his first gerbil building. He presented his design on paper one Saturday night over plates of spaghetti.

"Just how do you propose paying for this little empire of yours?" Mom challenged. We were all quiet, seeing who could suck down the longest noodle without chewing, little Phil occasionally choking as he tried to outdo Donald.

"The same way I buy socks, refrigerators, and anything else we need," Dad said. "With my Sears card."

"How much?"

"Probably about ten thousand," Dad said, pulling a second piece of paper out of his briefcase and showing the numbers to her.

"My God," Mom said. Her face went pale. "We'll be in debt the rest of our lives."

Dad scoffed at this. "I have a business plan," he said.

Mom pushed her plate aside. It was still piled high with spaghetti; she'd been eating less and was thinner than I'd ever seen her. I pulled her plate over to my side of the table and dug my fork in. I was growing taller, and I was even thinner than my mother; I was so hungry all of the time that Mom accused me of having a tapeworm.

Now Mom sighed and said, "You know, I never minded it that you wanted to keep a few gerbils. You get such a kick out of them, and I thought they'd keep you busy when you got out of the Navy. But I wasn't really thinking of gerbils as a second career."

"You never were much of a planner," Dad said. "What did you think I was going to do?"

"I don't know," Mom admitted, raising her hands in surrender. "I guess it was all sort of nebulous until now. Now it's happening."

"Darn right," Dad said.

Mom sighed. "Just promise to put your building where I can't see it from the house. I don't even want to *think* about gerbils."

~

PARTLY to appease my mother, but mainly to hide what he was doing, Dad chose the far southwest corner of our property for his first gerbil building, a spot hidden from the world by a thick stand of maples and oaks. An excavator came and created a long dirt road, and we all hiked the length of it to marvel at the barrel of the concrete truck spinning around and around to spill an endless waterfall of liquid cement into the frame Dad had built on the ground.

Later that month, a Sears truck delivered stacks of iron beams, sheet-metal siding, and fifty-pound bags of bolts. Dad hired a mason to put bolts in the beams at prescribed intervals. He also hired a plumber and an electrician. But he put up the bulk of the building himself, working alongside Donald and Grandfather every weekend to turn the piles, boxes, and bags of metal into a long, low structure about the size of our old ranch house in Virginia. He worked even through the start of deer hunting season, when hunters were stomping about in the state land around our property in their orange vests, firing bullets into the trees. The hunters seemed to have trouble distinguishing between deer and horses, or even between deer and chickens, because bullets were fired at our animals more times than we cared to count. Mom made us all stay inside the cleared areas of our stable and garden.

Once, a bullet came zinging out of the woods and ricocheted next to Dad as he straddled the very top of the new gerbil building, screwing on the metal roof. Mom happened to be standing below him because she'd brought his lunch.

"Will you please get down!" she yelled at Dad. "You're like a sitting duck up there! At least wait until Sunday when the hunters aren't out!"

"You never know how long good weather will hold," Dad argued back, and kept putting in screws.

It took nearly two months to complete the building. "Gosh, that wasn't too bad," Dad said as we all stood around to admire it. My father pulled a Navy handkerchief out of his back pocket and swabbed the sweat off his bald, sunburned head. "Good thing I played with so many Erector sets as a kid."

A year after our arrival in Massachusetts, the gerbils finally had a home of their own.

Chapter Thirteen

The Man Without a Nose

One resident of Tumblebrook Farm

CREDIT: D. G. ROBINSON JR.

In his self-published booklet, *Raise Gerbils as Pets, Laboratory Animals,* my dad's post-Navy business plan sounded simple: "Starting with two pairs of gerbils and two cages . . . you are 'in business' if the gerbils breed and you can sell them."

Thanks to his deal with Victor Schwentker, we had everything necessary to start peddling gerbils on a large scale within a year of moving to Massachusetts, including cages, racks, food, filing cabinets, watering carts, and, of course, gerbils—well over a thousand of them within that first year. But the single most essential item Dad acquired from Victor wasn't something he ferried home in a U-Haul from Brant Lake, though, but a single piece of paper. On it was a list of Victor's clients. These included the Department of Defense, the National Institutes of Health, Johns Hopkins University, Harvard University, and several pharmaceutical companies.

One day, as I was filling water bottles and feeders in the gerbil building, my father reminded me that no matter how many lucky breaks you get in business, you can't ever take things for granted. "Your luck can run dry any minute," Dad said. "For instance, a lot of people would expect an animal-raising venture to be a self-sustaining business. You might think that breeding animals is like having a factory, and that a profitable product would appear in a steady stream with very little effort."

This was seldom the case, though, Dad warned, "even if gerbils may seem to approach this ideal. As in any other business, you really have to know your market and stay ahead of the curve."

By the time our gerbil colony was established, scientists had already been using rodents as disease models for decades. In Dad's eyes, any laboratory researcher who already relied on mice, rats, or hamsters as research subjects was a potential convert to gerbils. Gerbils might even prove to be valuable for certain studies that scientists couldn't conduct with other rodents. This could translate into sizeable profits.

"Did you know," Dad enthused over his briefcase of papers at the dinner table one night, "that of the sixty-six thousand laboratory animals used in this country daily, over ninety-five percent are rodents?"

"I had no idea," Mom said. "It's amazing how many things I don't know."

As usual, Dad either missed or ignored her sarcasm; I could never be sure which it was with him. He kept talking as if nobody had said a word. "All we have to do to succeed is find a niche market for gerbils," Dad assured us. "Give me a niche to fill, and I'll do it."

Thanks to my father's steady marketing efforts, which included advertisements in laboratory magazines and direct mailings, gerbils began inching their way into research studies on epilepsy, stroke, nutrition, human behavior, and infectious diseases those first two years on the farm. In a fit of optimism,

Dad even created his own letterhead. The letterhead read "Tumblebrook Farm, Home of the Gerbil" in English and, in tiny letters below a simple line drawing of a house, the same thing in Mandarin Chinese.

"Why Chinese?" I asked Dad, squinting at the letters.

"For the gerbils," he said, sounding surprised. "It's the language of their homeland."

~

DONALD and I both worked for Dad after school and on weekends. Some days, it seemed like it took us years to trudge up to the silver building that sat like a windowless ranch house out on the back ten acres, especially in cold weather or when we were trying to outrun the mosquitoes. While our friends played sports or watched TV, we went to work and came back with wood shavings in our hair and stinking of gerbil pee. The stinging smell of rodent urine was so bad that Donald, assigned the unlucky job of loading the jeep full of used gerbil shavings for Grandfather to drive to the dump, rechristened that vehicle the "Honey Wagon."

Our chores in the gerbil building were mundane enough to produce the sort of altered state that I imagined my musician idols, Morrison and Hendrix, achieved with drugs. As Dad's radio hummed easy-listening music in the background, we wheeled our carts up and down the cement aisles, rhythmically doling out green food pellets, filling water bottles, and cleaning out cages.

We also tagged new litters of squirming, pink, blind gerbil pups as we moved through the tall walls of cages. Dad used a special system to track new litters. This involved attaching color-coded plastic rings to the cages of breeding pairs to mark the ages of the babies and recording births on index cards. The colored rings—red, green, blue, or yellow—each represented a certain age in weeks.

We weaned the pups at five weeks, and the colored rings made it easy to identify which gerbils were ready to leave their mothers. We separated the new weanlings by sex into larger metal cages that held fifty or so at a time. I hated the assembly-line nature of the work, and tried to think of these gangs of young, single-sex gerbils as teenagers in school dormitories, waiting to grow up and get married. Dad had a more pragmatic view.

"It's pretty much like propagating seeds," he observed. "You just put the gerbils in a box and watch them grow. When they're old enough to breed, you set them out in new boxes of their own."

Though the work was often mind-numbing, my dad's gerbil hothouse provided me with a welcome sanctuary after fending for myself at the high school, especially if it was an afternoon where I was lucky enough to work alone. Often I'd linger there after my chores were done, soothed by the steady scratching noises of the animals in their shavings. I'd change the radio station from Dad's elevator music to rock and roll—forbidden by my father, who was afraid that hippie music would upset the animals.

Occasionally I even brought homework and did it at Dad's metal desk in the corner. Dad's desk was "strictly off-limits to all employees," that is, Donald and me. But I loved sitting there and, if I finished my homework, flipping through the science journals that collected in dusty knee-high stacks all around the floor. In this way, I discovered that there were pygmy gerbils, bushy-tailed gerbils, fat-tailed gerbils, Egyptian gerbils, Indian hairy-footed gerbils, and naked-soled gerbils. I wanted to see and hold them all.

I also found out that our own Mongolian gerbils weren't technically gerbils at all but a type of jird. They were also called desert rats, antelope rats, yellow rats, or clawed jirds, and fell in the order of rodents (Rodentia) and in the same suborder as mice and rats (Myomorpha). Gerbils were in the same family as hamsters (Cricetidae), but despite my mother's dislike of them, I thought gerbils were cuter. I loved the thick black tufts at the ends of their tails and their dun color. The color, which Dad called "agouti," was the same lovely soft brown as the cotton-tailed rabbits I often startled on my long walk up the dirt road to the gerbilry from our house.

One day at breakfast, I asked Dad if I could have some gerbils to keep as pets in my bedroom. I'd loved training Kinky in Virginia, and I hated Dad's view that all gerbils were the same, just "drones," as he put it. I wanted to prove him wrong and show him that gerbils had souls.

But Dad refused. "Absolutely not!" he shouted, clearly panicked by the very idea. "You are barred from bringing any gerbils into the house, and that's an order! Is that clear?"

"But why, Dad?" I asked, truly puzzled. I knew that he wouldn't miss the ones I took. He certainly didn't notice when Donald carried a shoebox of gerbils on his bike to sell to local kids for spare change, a practice he would continue through college, when he sometimes bartered gerbils for beer. "You know I'd take good care of them."

"That's not the issue," he said. "You kids would bring them down to the house, and then you'd get tired of them. Next thing I know, your pets would be back at the gerbil building, contaminating the colony with fleas or disease, and we'd be ruined. Ruined! Do you hear me?"

"What disease could the gerbils catch if Holly brought them to the house?" Mom intervened from the stove, where she was scrambling eggs. "The children don't have any diseases. I don't, either." She looked pointedly at my father.

Dad shook his head. "Sally, you don't know that. A staph infection could spread like wildfire through the gerbils and wipe out the business. Or fleas! Did you ever think of fleas, and what that would do to the gerbils? I'd never sell another animal if I ever filled an order with flea-infested or sick animals. We may never be a germ-free colony, but I can at least keep the colony clean."

Mom scoffed. "If you're really so worried about our children infecting your gerbils, maybe you should put a shower inside the gerbil building so the kids can wash up before they go in there to do all of that work for you," she said, turning back to the pan of eggs. "Hell," she muttered into the stove hood, "why not make us all wear spacesuits? Life with you can't get much weirder than it already is."

~

Two years after our arrival in Massachusetts, Dad retired from the Navy without fanfare after twenty years of service. He immediately incorporated Tumblebrook Farm as a business and named himself president and treasurer. Mom was listed as company secretary. Donald and I were official company employees, "on the books," Dad told us proudly, our work hours and pay meticulously recorded.

I didn't mind being a tax write-off. But being an employee meant mandatory attendance at Tumblebrook Farm company meetings. These were held in the dining room every Sunday night without fail, in case the IRS ever dropped by to see Dad's accounts, which he kept in oversized record books that looked like something out of a Charles Dickens novel. All he needed was a pair of fingerless gloves.

"I don't get why we have to attend," I grumbled as I helped Mom load the dishwasher before one company meeting. "It's not like Dad ever asks us for an opinion."

"Your father misses his Navy staff meetings," Mom said. "Humor him."

That night, Dad opened up the company meeting in the dining room with a cigarette and a cup of coffee at his elbow and his briefcase in front of him. He began with an official welcome, then said, "My intention tonight is to bring you up to speed on the current state of affairs and inform you of coming events." He passed out a printed agenda.

We heard a detailed update on building maintenance and construction. Then came a report on sales, which had been brisk again that week. Finally Dad surprised us.

"I'm proud to announce that we can now promote Tumblebrook Farm as the world's largest producer of gerbils," he told us. "Our monthly sales now surpass those of any other gerbil breeder, including what Victor used to do." He gazed at each of us in turn, as if waiting for us to dispute his numbers. When we didn't, he argued back anyway.

"It's an entirely truthful tag line, unlike some," Dad said, casting a sidelong glance at a copy of *Lab Animal Magazine* lying next to his briefcase, a look that said, *You know who you are*. "Given our rapid rise to success, I have begun plans for phase two of the business, which involves the construction of a second building similar in size to the first."

"You've got to be kidding," Mom said. She gripped her coffee cup so hard that her knuckles went white. "We don't have that kind of money."

"We have no choice," Dad said. "Despite the success of Tumblebrook Farm as a supplier of gerbils worldwide, there can be no resting on our laurels. We still have to grow while watching every penny."

"Dad, shouldn't Grandmother and Grandfather be downstairs to hear this, too?" I asked. "They do an awful lot of work around here."

My father ignored me. "As I was saying," he went on, "we can expect to have to tighten our belts during the next phase of the company's expansion."

This was a common refrain at our company meetings. Phrases like "we'll have to tighten our belts," "trim around the edges," and "lower the heat" were so routine that Donald, Philip, and I immediately began fidgeting, kicking at each other beneath the dining room table and dropping bits of food to make the dogs start fighting. Meanwhile, Mom stubbed out a Benson and Hedges on top of Dad's Camels in the ashtray and gave a longing glance at the paperback novel she'd left on the sideboard.

"Still, despite our need to proceed with the utmost caution as we venture into phase two of the business, I've deemed it necessary to hire additional staff," Dad announced. "You kids simply aren't keeping up with the work."

I looked at Donald. I knew who skimped on cleaning cages. He made a face and kicked me under the table again.

"Who in the world is going to work for you?" Mom asked.

"Your mother, for a start," Dad said.

That got us. We all stopped fidgeting, even Mom. "In the gerbil building?" I asked, trying to picture Grandmother, perfectly coiffed and outfitted in one of her proper tweed suits, taking that long walk up the dirt road to scrub out pee-soaked cages.

"No, of course not," Dad said, irritated that we were all giggling, even Mom. "I've made Grandmother our new company secretary."

"Oh, thank God," Mom said. "I've been fired at last. I don't suppose there's any severance package, though. Ah well." She stood up, carrying her coffee mug with her.

"Where are you going?" Dad asked in alarm.

"I assume that my presence is no longer required at company meetings, now that I've been given the boot," Mom said, and left the room without even waiting for permission to be excused, grabbing her book off the sideboard as she made her getaway.

~

ONCE he'd added Grandmother to the gerbil payroll, Dad put a telephone extension in her apartment so that she could field orders from customers while she continued to cook, sew, do housework, and take care of Philip when Mom was busy.

Occasionally I'd wander into Grandmother's apartment

and overhear her taking down a message in her tidy retail clerk's hand on the pad next to her new flesh-tone telephone. Grandmother's keen interest in people, retail experience, good manners, and vaguely British accent made her the perfect public relations representative for Tumblebrook Farm. She'd chuckle over a Swedish researcher's joke, or ask a Maryland scientist about his daughter's wedding, and then she'd get right down to business, persuading scientists around the world that they really didn't want to be caught short on gerbils, so it was always best to order a few spares.

"What do you tell your friends about your new job, Grandmother?" I asked her one afternoon. "Do they know what Dad does?"

"Of course they know," Grandmother answered crisply. "I'm not the least bit ashamed. You shouldn't be, either. I think your father's done very well for himself. So does the rest of the family. Your uncle Skip and uncle Don both say they'd give their eyeteeth to build a business for themselves the way your father has. Most people don't have the nerve to start a business from scratch."

"But do you tell your friends at church about the gerbils?" I pressed.

"Oh, my, yes," she said, tearing a message off her pink telephone pad. "And let me tell you, they're all very impressed. They've never heard of gerbils, most of them, you know. They can't even begin to imagine how we have thousands of them up here. But not one of my friends has ever expressed any reservations about it."

"Nobody?" I asked, surprised.

"Oh, well, once in a while, I suppose," Grandmother said,

patting her hair. "But then I point out how very useful gerbils are for the different diseases these scientists are working so hard to cure, like cancer and epilepsy, and people understand that."

"They do?"

"Of course they do!" Grandmother stood up and went over to the refrigerator, where she began pulling out ingredients for a shepherd's pie. "Not that I tell just anyone," she admitted. "When Laura and I took the bus to Boston with the senior citizens' center, the bus driver asked me if I was retired, because I'm so young looking." Here Grandmother paused, savoring that comment and patting her hair once more before going on. "I told him, 'Oh, my, no, I'm not retired. I still work as a telephone secretary.' "

I laughed, trying to imagine what the bus driver might have said if she'd told him about the gerbils. "That sure was quick thinking, Grammy," I said.

She nodded. "Yes, well, not everyone needs to know our business, do they?"

~

WITHIN a year of incorporating Tumblebrook Farm, Dad was able to complete construction on his second building. We now had more than two thousand gerbils, many of them producing new litters every month. We were shipping gerbils to university research laboratories, medical schools, government scientists, and pharmaceutical companies all over the world. This meant that we were not only cleaning cages, feeding, watering, and weaning animals but also boxing them up and driving them to the airport once or twice each week.

To keep up with business, Dad began hiring maintenance

workers and animal caretakers. Donald and I met Dad's first outside employee, Jack Baptiste, when we showed up at the gerbil building one Monday afternoon to clean cages. "This is our new animal caretaker," Dad said, clapping Jack on the shoulder with the zeal of a feudal lord congratulating a peasant for fields well plowed. "He'll be helping your grandfather, too, with all-around maintenance handiwork, trips to the airport, and whatnot."

Jack was a tall, knock-kneed man whose face was a road map of burst blood vessels. His skinny arms bulged with ropy blue veins and Popeye muscles. He wore a faded pair of blue work pants and black boots, but his tattered denim shirt had been starched and ironed with knife-edge creases. For the ten years that Jack worked for us, I never once saw him without a crisply starched shirt.

But Jack's single most unique feature was his nose, or rather, his lack of one. Where his nose had been was just a flap of skin between two nostrils, giving Jack the pinched look of a flounder glaring up at you from the bottom of the ocean.

"You see how I am so strong?" he asked me in his heavy French accent that afternoon while we worked together, cleaning cages and feeding the gerbils. "Me, I was a logger in Quebec." He made a muscle to show me how he'd felled trees, possibly without an ax.

I focused on Jack's bulging muscle to avoid staring at his nose. "You're very strong," I said.

"Strong like mad bull," he agreed with satisfaction.

"Why did you stop logging?" I asked.

Jack shrugged. "The trees, they all go away, too many. And it is so cold in Quebec, you know? You always need your dancing to keep you warm. Dancing and a fiddle, and a crossbow to keep the bears away."

"Was your wife living up there with you?" I asked.

"No, no, no! No women in the woods of Quebec," he assured me. "They bleed, the bears come. No good. But you dance with the other loggers, you can stay warm anyhow."

Before coming to work for my father, Jack had been an animal caretaker on a chicken farm. "I quit there, because they have this buyer, he come to buy the sick or dead birds for the soups because they so damn cheap," Jack said. "That is bad thing to do, I know that, so I quit."

Eventually Mom took notice of Jack's shirts and began taking some of her laundry to Jack's wife, Louisa. I loved driving over to Jack's house with my mother because it was like no other place I'd ever seen.

Jack and Louisa lived on a potholed dirt road in a crooked cartoon house with a stovepipe chimney and red asbestos siding. They kept their own little animal colonies on the side. They sold rabbits for meat. They also bred domestic animals to sell as pets: Maine coon cats, with tufted ears and broad, Cheshire-cat faces; foxy-faced Pomeranians with plumed tails and barks that could shatter glass; and homing pigeons that Jack kissed on the tops of their little heads before setting them free to fly who knew where. Mom called their farm "the little French village."

Louisa was built like a bullet and smelled of cat piss and dandelion wine. Because she made a living by taking in other people's laundry, their yard was a spiderweb of laundry lines with clothes that flapped and slapped at your face and shoulders whenever you tried to make your way to the front door. Louisa also crocheted sweaters and blankets in color combinations that made you squint: yellow with purple and orange, brown with orange and green, orange with mauve and pink. Orange was the one consistent color theme in that house.

Each time we visited, Louisa showed us her handmade items, sliding her creations out of clear plastic bags as tenderly as if they were babies being unwrapped from layettes.

"You like?" she asked every time, hopeful of a sale.

Finally, I felt so sorry for her that I bought a sweater with my babysitting money, a brown and green and orange cardigan.

"You'll never wear that thing," Mom said as we drove away. "It doesn't pay to feel sorry for people."

"You don't know," I argued. "I might wear it on a really, really cold day."

"Let me know in advance," Mom said. "I'll want to take your picture."

But cold weather came and went, and I never did put on that sweater. Louisa's creation remained in its plastic sack under my bed until I went to college, its brown bulk as shiny as a bear, startling me each time I looked under the bed for something else and reminding me of Canada and the men who danced together there, trying to stay warm.

~

IT TURNED out that Jack Baptiste was a lucky find. As Dad's gerbils increased in number and he began looking for other animal caretakers, he discovered that it was nearly impossible to attract and keep responsible employees. If you looked in the local weekly paper, there were always three ads sure to be found under the jobs column: dishwashers at the local inn, line workers at the wire factory, and animal handlers at Tumblebrook Farm. This never changed in the twenty-five years that my father raised gerbils.

Dad did everything he could to beat good people out of the bushes. He tried offering more than minimum wage. He even paid for employee health benefits over Mom's protests.

"That's crazy. You won't even let me buy curtains for the family room," Mom said. "How can we afford to pay other people's doctor bills?"

"Some of these people have families," he told her. "What are they supposed to do if their kids get sick?"

To sweeten the deal, Dad offered his workers an added incentive: a quarter more per hour if they stopped smoking, despite the fact that he continued to run through a couple of packs of Camels a day.

Still, despite these perks, our employees were not always the top-quality individuals that Dad might have hoped for. Picture the people you see every day working the counters of your favorite fast-food places or sweeping floors at the mall. Now double or halve their ages, give each one a drug or alcohol habit, dress them in Salvation Army finds, add a twitch here and a blind eye or a limp there, and that would pretty much describe most of the employees at Tumblebrook Farm.

We hired thieves and wife beaters, the wives who got beaten, junkies and alcoholics, hitchhikers passing through, and teenagers whose cars roared like lions and were held together by duct tape. Dad's employees typically were, as Mom so succinctly put it, "beneath the bottom of the barrel."

Most employees gladly accepted the quarter-an-hour quit-smoking raise and then stood around smoking under the ceiling fans in the gerbil buildings to avoid detection whenever they lit up. Among the men, one was an ex-junkie who added a dozen spoonfuls of sugar to each cup of coffee and was perfectly happy carrying on conversations alone. Another was a Civil War buff who occasionally showed up to clean cages dressed as Johnny Reb, while a third fellow was a self-described "unemployed environmentalist" who wrapped himself naked around a tree in order to keep a local farmer from cutting it down.

Among the women, one called herself Daisy Mae and dressed for work in cutoff shorts that showed two half moons of her ass no matter what the weather; she made the rounds among the male employees and managed to get them to do most of her work while she napped in the sun out on the picnic table that Dad had put outside the gerbil building to boost company morale through impromptu employee picnics. Another woman had to leave without notice anytime her enraged husband figured out that she was back working for us and came charging up the road in his souped-up Chevy truck, a rifle aimed out the window.

Still, despite their flaws, Dad always expected the best of his workers, especially the women. He claimed that female employees did better work than the men, and given a choice—a rare day—he would always hire a female applicant over a man.

"Why?" I asked him one afternoon as he and Mom and I gathered to watch *General Hospital*. One of the few perks of working for ourselves was that we never had to miss our favorite TV shows, even in an era before TiVo and VCRs.

"Women don't get bored doing repetitive tasks," Dad

explained. "Plus, their maternal instincts really kick in around the gerbils."

Mom shook her head, not taking her eyes off the television. "What about me?" she asked. "I get bored easily and I hate gerbils."

"You've always been different," Dad said.

~

ONE day after school, I walked up to the gerbil building to clean cages with Angeline, a stout bottle blonde in her fifties. Angeline's gum-snapping, no-nonsense approach to work meant that she and I could complete our list of required tasks—posted each day by my father on the bulletin board by the door—in the shortest time possible. Then we could lounge around and chat.

I liked working with Angeline. She talked to me as if I were thirty, not fifteen, and asked my advice on everything from boyfriends to buying a secondhand car. In this way, I was like everyone else in my family: willing to give advice to anybody, even if I had to ad-lib.

That afternoon, Angeline and I spent four hours doing the usual: cleaning six racks of cages with twenty-four cages per rack. We put the gerbils in cages filled with fresh shavings by other employees the night before, then pushed the dirty cages on wheeled carts down to the washroom. There we scraped the contents into trash barrels and washed the cages at waist-high industrial sinks, soaking them in disinfectant and rinsing them until they gleamed. When the cages were finally clean enough to suit Dad's daily inspection, we wheeled them over to the drying racks, where we left the cages for someone else to fill with clean shavings the next day.

"Doesn't it seem weird to you," I asked Angeline, "that Dad keeps breeding the same gerbils to each other? I mean, isn't it like incest or something? Shouldn't the babies all be retarded? I thought that's what happened when brothers and sisters got married."

"The idea is to standardize the line," Angeline explained. "If you keep the genetics the same from one generation to the next, you start weeding out variables that can show up in experiments and give some poor little researcher a heart attack. That's why scientists have been inbreeding different mice for decades." She cracked her gum, considering. "Your dad must have over a dozen generations of gerbils by now," she calculated with an excitement I couldn't fathom. "All descended from the same ancestors he bought from Victor Schwentker."

"Do you ever feel bad about working here?" I asked. At fifteen, I had reached the "wallowing age," as Mom called it.

Angeline shook her head. "Not at all. Your dad takes good care of his animals, and I know there are scientists out there doing stroke research with the gerbils. My dad died of a stroke."

I thought about this as I picked up the next gerbil. How many gerbil deaths would I accept if I knew those deaths would bring a cure for someone with cystic fibrosis, like my sister? What was an animal's life worth compared to a human's? I didn't know the answer. I only knew that talking about gerbils and medical research was a lot different from holding a gerbil in my hand and feeling it, so warm and yet nearly weightless, an animal with a heartbeat of its own.

"He's coming!" one of the other workers shrieked suddenly from the other end of the building, where she'd been doling out green pellets from the food cart. "The commander is on his way. I can see him from the end door!"

Unlike in his military days, when Dad had hidden the fact that he was raising gerbils, here in his gerbil kingdom he relied upon his Navy title to convey an extra mantle of authority. Every one of his employees called him "the commander."

The window in the door offered the only view of the dirt road leading up to the gerbil building. Someone in the building was always posted there as a lookout to alert other employees when my father was approaching. That way, they had plenty of time to turn the thermostat back down in winter, if one of the employees had brazenly cranked up the heat. They could also scramble out from under the fan if they'd been smoking cigarettes, or climb off the picnic table outside if they'd gotten high and needed a nap. We always had plenty of time to appear busy because Dad took forever to actually reach the building.

I wandered over to the door and peered out. Dad was walking as he always did, with his head down and his hands in his pockets, so deep in thought that he hunched his shoulders and moved as slowly as if he were dragging a bag of gerbil pellets up the road behind him. I wondered what he was thinking about, and realized I didn't have a clue.

Chapter Fourteen

My Mom Wears Jodhpurs

Sniffles, the meanest pony in the world

CREDIT: THE HOLLY ROBINSON COLLECTION

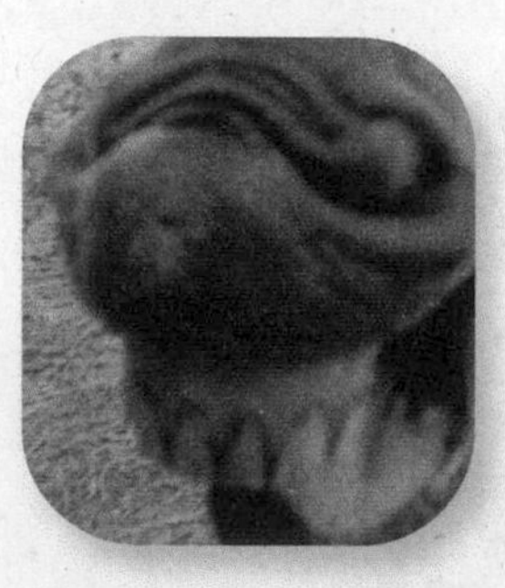

Mom hadn't held a job since marrying my father, but this didn't faze her a bit. "It's time I went back to work," she announced one night at dinner. "I'm going to give riding lessons."

"You can't do that. You don't know a single thing about teaching," Dad said.

She shrugged. "I've been getting on and off horses all my life, haven't I? All I have to do is show other people how."

Dad succeeded in business because he left nothing to chance and followed every rule in the book. Mom succeeded because she thought every chance was worth taking. If she didn't like the rules, she made up her own. For instance, when she failed her driver's test in Virginia, she immediately drove to a different city and took it again. When we moved to Massachusetts, Mom signed up for ballet lessons. After being told that she was too old to dance en pointe, she practiced for hours on end until she was up on toe shoes for the first time at age thirty-nine.

Mom derived her confidence in part from her beauty. At age sixteen, when she came into the kitchen to show her father and his friend her new prom dress, Grandfather's friend had cocked an eyebrow and said, "Everett, that girl looks like something you can't afford."

By the time we moved to Massachusetts, Mom was in her late thirties but had the trim, athletic build of a much younger woman and dark hair without a strand of silver. "Well, why shouldn't I be a ballerina?" she asked me, tiptoeing around the living room in her new pink satin toe shoes. "I look good in a leotard. Better than some of those high school girls who can't keep their hands out of the cookie jar."

Once Mom made up her mind to run a riding stable, we rarely saw her in anything but formfitting canary-yellow jodhpurs and knee-high black boots. She even wore her jodhpurs and boots to pick me up at school, to collect Grandmother's prescriptions at the pharmacy, or to dash into the grocery store for milk and eggs.

"I think of my jodhpurs as my calling card," she told me when I asked why she didn't change her clothes. "People see me in this outfit and ask where I ride, and I can tell them that I give riding lessons. They almost always call me."

With her exotic outfit, drop-dead figure, dark hair, and quick smile, it was no wonder they called. In her jodhpurs and boots, Mom made men forget their own names when she walked by. I once saw a woman whack her husband with a purse over my mother.

The barn was finished, but if Mom was really going into business full-time, we needed a riding ring, too. We built it the same way we'd done everything else on the farm: with salvaged materials and our own labor. Donald dragged additional lumber over from the state land and we put up a circular rail fence in a matter of days.

And then, every day after school for three weeks, Donald and I dug rocks out of the soil with shovels and our bare hands, the heat beating down on our necks and making us dizzy, the effort of removing the rocks gradually shaving our fingernails down to black slivers.

"Now I know where the settlers got all those rocks for their stone walls," Donald groaned at one point.

"And their foundations," I said, heaving a small boulder into the back of the tractor cart. "Don't forget all of those stone foundations."

The effort was worth it, though: when we were finished, the riding ring was impressive, with its white rail fence and smooth dirt surface. The ring doubled as a paddock for turning out the horses or exercising them on lunge lines for people who boarded their horses with us.

Gradually, as Mom built up her business, I began spending more of my working hours in the stable than in the gerbil buildings. This suited me fine. The gerbils were kept in nearly windowless, climate-controlled, claustrophobic metal ranch houses. Two hours spent tending gerbils left me with my eyes burning from the ammonia and my skin itching from the sawdust. But the barn was a lovely place that smelled of hay and molasses, horses and saddle soap.

The gerbils ran from my touch when I lifted the lids of their cages. When I appeared in the stables, the horses came to the doors of their stalls and nodded in welcome, snorting and pushing their velvety muzzles in my direction for a treat from my pocket. I talked to the horses the same way I talked to the gerbils, but I could count on certain horses answering back, whinnying or stomping their hooves.

There were a lot of cats in the barn, too. People dropped them off in the middle of the night sometimes. There were cats of all sizes and colors, and they did their own talking as they followed me up and down the aisles, arching their backs or rubbing against my boots as they waited for me to fill their food dishes in the tack room.

In the gerbil building, I was subjected to my father's critical eye and constant scoldings about waste, money, and the terror of fleas. But in the stable, I felt welcomed and useful as I fed the horses before school and turned them out into the pastures with a thundering of hooves. I loved to watch the horses run with heads and tails held high, looking as if they might, at any moment, take wing.

~

WHAT is it about girls and horses? People love to equate the passion that young girls have for horses with burgeoning sexuality, but girls who ride know that true horse lust is all about power.

Within a year of opening her riding school, Mom had collected a group of enthusiastic barn rats, girls whose zealous affection for horses was equal to my own. The girls never minded helping us shovel out stalls, fill water buckets, or comb burrs out of tails.

To these girls, I was a TV idol. I gradually learned to enjoy living up to their high expectations by fearlessly climbing onto even the most headstrong horses to help train them. One particular resident horse—a sorrel half-Thoroughbred colt appropriately named Derringer—was completely psychotic. Anytime someone mounted him, Derringer would take off like a bullet, head low to the ground, body flattened so that your only chance for survival was to press your body against his neck. Finally, I broke him of this by pulling his nose toward my knee and nearly flipping us both onto the ground.

The stable was the one place in my life where I felt in control. It was also a place where age meant nothing. Women and girls who love horses have a natural common ground, and I found myself in demand as a riding partner on the trails. I didn't have many friends at school, but there was always someone to talk to at the barn, so I was much less lonely than before. School became something I had to get through before riding.

Joanne and Mystique were among my mother's first riding students. They lived together in an apartment overlooking the Catholic church in town with a fuzzball of a gray dog that was perpetually panting, no matter what the weather. Mystique was a philosophy professor at Radcliffe College, and Joanne had a little leather shop in Brookfield, where she made belts and sandals and handbags for the tourists who came apple picking or leaf peeping through central Massachusetts.

It took us a while to catch on to the fact that Joanne and Mystique were a couple, despite the fact that both of them sheared their hair shorter than my brother Donald's and dressed in identical blue jeans and T-shirts. Once we did, though, we accepted them as they were. Mom shared her coffee every morning with Joanne as they watched the horses in the back pasture, and Dad liked to linger at the kitchen table whenever the women rode in the ring, since neither wore a bra.

Joanne was a sumo wrestler of a woman with serious dark eyes and sleek black hair. She was one of the first eight adults to sign up for riding lessons when Mom started offering beginner classes for adults. For that lesson, I helped Mom tack up the gentle school horses we'd picked up at auctions and loop their reins over the top rail of the ring. Mom instructed the nervous women to stand at their horses' heads while I demonstrated how to mount a horse in the center of the ring.

"Hold the reins in your left hand and the pommel of the saddle in your right," Mom lectured. "Then lift your left leg—that's your *left* leg, Sandra, otherwise you'll end up sitting backward—and put your left foot in the stirrup."

The women all dutifully took hold of their reins and saddles. Unfortunately, the lesson was cut short when one of the barn cats, a black and white tom we called Rocky, flung himself kamikaze style off the top rail of the ring and onto the neck of one of the horses. Panic ensued. The horse that Rocky had speared with his claws reared back, tugging at the top rail and startling the other horses so that they pulled back, too.

The reins were only looped around the top rail, but they held fast. The collective strength of the horses was enough to pull the top board right off its fence posts, though; the horses set off with it and dragged the fence rail halfway across the ring before we managed to stop them.

The women screamed, terrifying the horses even more. In seconds, there were horses and reins and broken boards and cats and dust flying every which way, unsettling even my unflappable mother, who yelled, "Calm down! Please, all of you, if you calm down, the horses will, too!"

The noise caused my father to run up to the barn from the house, shouting something to my mother about lawsuits and lessons not being worth the risk. My mother was not dissuaded. It took us several minutes, but we eventually had all of the horses settled along the rail again. One by one, my mother taught the women how to mount their horses, and soon they were plodding around the ring, all of them looking pleased with themselves for not giving up.

Every woman there wanted to be my mother.

~

AMONG the boarders, the woman I rode with most often was Savage Jones, a former film agent married to a pediatrician. Savage was fiftysomething, but with her tight red curls, stocky build, and pink Keds sneakers, she looked like an eight-year-old girl on coffee, bouncing along on her toes beside her giant bay horse, Bongo. Savage always carried a mayonnaise jar filled with a clear liquid that she sipped throughout our trail rides.

"It's only vitamin water," she assured me. "You can never get enough water to flush out the poisons from your system."

Bongo had been gelded too late and was so wild that Savage appeared to fly around beside him like a trapeze artist dangling from the lead line. Yet she wouldn't ride him in the ring.

"Too many eyes watching," she confided. So I ended up leading Savage on trail rides through the woods, keeping Ladybug solidly in front of Bongo so that he couldn't take off.

One summer morning, Savage showed up at the stables wearing a flea collar. "There's no reason this wouldn't work on a human," Savage said, pulling the plastic collar a little tighter as we set off down the trail through the state land across the street.

Usually we followed the main logging road over tiny streams, beneath towering pines, and through an ancient orchard of gnarled, graying apple trees. One part of the trail was like a fairy-tale forest, with pine trees so tall and thick that nothing but moss grew in the damp blackness beneath them.

As we rode, Savage talked about her former life in New York. Her chatter was as constant as the deerflies that needled our faces and shoulders, forcing us to tuck branches into the horses' bridles and into our riding helmets for protection. Between Savage's constant monologue, the rocking horses, the buzzing flies, and the swishing branches, I'd be lulled nearly to sleep. So I was startled when one day Savage yanked Bongo to a halt in the middle of the path and cried, "I know. Let's have an adventure today!"

"What kind of adventure?" I asked uneasily. I trusted Savage about as much as I trusted her horse.

"How about taking this trail for a change?" Savage pointed at some flattened grass next to the logging road.

"That's just a deer path," I warned, but Savage had already turned Bongo away from Ladybug to nose through the thick brush.

Against my better judgment, I followed her; Mom had drilled it into me that my job was to safeguard the boarders. And so I was right behind Savage when her horse stumbled into a nest of digger wasps.

The wasps buzzed around Bongo and Savage in an angry mob. The horse reared and took off with Savage bouncing in the saddle like a rag doll. I spurred Ladybug after the bigger horse; half Arabian, Ladybug was fast, surefooted, and very determined. She caught up with the bigger gelding easily and I leaned over to grab the other horse's reins, which Savage had dropped while she was making sounds like a fleet of fire trucks.

Once we'd halted, Savage righted herself in the saddle,

adjusted her flea collar, and gave me a shaky smile. She hadn't dropped the mayonnaise jar. Now she lifted it to her lips. "You know, maybe Bongo is too much horse for me," she said. "He's just like my husband."

~

BEFORE long, Mom had accrued so many riding students that she had to hire an assistant teacher. She spent some of her earnings on an indoor riding arena—a metal building that was like a huge, empty gerbil building—and, between boarders and school horses, stabled over forty horses at a time.

Yet Mom was still restless. "I think I'll breed Arabians," she declared. "I've always loved their pointy little ears and muzzles, and the way they run with their tails in the air like fountains."

"You can't do that. You don't know one thing about breeding horses," Dad argued.

She shrugged. "I'm sure the horses know what to do," she said.

Mom bought a chestnut Arabian stallion named Nahill and had me help her train him. As long as there were no mares within smelling distance, Nahill was personable enough. His nastiest habit was nipping our pockets in search of treats and pinching our skin by mistake; I cured him of this by biting him on the ear. Before long, he was so tame that Nahill would trot by my side on a lead line as we hopped over rails on the ground together.

But breeding horses wasn't as easy as breeding gerbils. You couldn't just let a stallion run loose with a mare, Mom explained, or the mare might get hurt because the stallion was too forceful.

Our first attempt at breeding Nahill was with Justice, an Arabian mare that a woman from Springfield boarded at our stable; Justice's owner wanted a foal to train for her son. We waited for Justice to show the edgy signs of being in heat, and then Mom asked me to cross-tie the mare in the riding arena.

When Mom led Nahill out of the barn and into the echoing metal arena, I was startled to see our playful stallion transformed into a head-tossing, rearing beast, snorting and pawing the ground because he'd scented the mare. With a roar, he launched himself at the mare's rump, breaking free of Mom's hold on his lead line. The stallion reared and mounted the mare.

Justice's eyes rolled until the whites showed. She tried to spin around to escape the stallion, but the ropes held. Nahill's penis dropped from its shaft, as long as my arm and bright pink. I was nearly as terrified as the mare.

"Mom!" I cried. "He's going to hurt her!" I made a move to release the cross ties, but Mom grabbed me just in time.

"Stay back," she ordered. "This is how it's got to be done. Don't worry. It'll be over in seconds."

It was. The stallion gripped the mare's quivering sides with his front hooves for a moment more. Then Nahill groaned and collapsed on top of her, nearly toppling the smaller horse beneath him.

Mom shoved at Nahill's sweat-foamed shoulder to get him off the mare and led the staggering stallion back to his stall. I untied Justice as quickly as my shaking hands would allow.

The mare was suddenly, oddly calm, almost sleepy. I fed her a carrot in the flat of my hand.

The pregnancy took. And, amazingly, we were all there to watch Justice give birth. This, too, was much different from what I'd seen in the gerbil building.

It was a Saturday afternoon, and Joanne and Mystique were at the barn. So were Savage and her pediatrician husband, Whitney. Mom stood next to the stall door with them while Joanne, Mystique, and I climbed into the hayloft for a better view.

Nothing happened for a long time. The mare lay on her side, then stood up, then threw herself back down on the stall floor. Justice whinnied now and then and lifted her head. Finally her sides began to heave at regular intervals. I started to feel frightened; the horse looked as if she were in pain but trying to sleep through it. Her enormous dark eyes were glazed and unblinking.

When the foal began to crown, Mom went into the stall and kneeled beside Justice's head, stroking the horse's neck, which by now had foamed with sweat. Eventually the foal emerged. As it did, Justice lifted her head and whinnied again.

To my astonishment, the foal, though still halfway in its mother's body, nickered back. Spurred on by the murmur of sound, Justice pushed once more and the foal slid free. I started to cry, for no reason I could explain, and Joanne and Mystique both put their arms around me, wiping tears away as well.

In less than half an hour, the mare and foal were both on their feet, and the foal was nuzzling its mother for milk. The foal was black with one white sock and a white blaze down the length of its nose.

"Must be a boy, if he's on his feet already," Whitney crowed. "Look at him. So strong! What a boy!"

Next to me in the loft, Joanne wiped her eyes and made a scissoring motion with her fingers, then pointed to Whitney. "Some men would be better off as geldings," she whispered.

~

THROUGH the years, only one man ever boarded his horse with us. This was Francis, the nineteen-year-old son of a dentist and the owner of an elegant Appaloosa quarterhorse gelding. Francis quickly won my mother's admiration and tried hard to win mine.

Francis had only one aspiration in life, and that was to be a cowboy. While we all used lightweight, flat English saddles, he rode in a heavy, hand-tooled Western saddle over a Navajo blanket. Francis kept a rope hanging from the saddle's tall pommel and could lasso a running dog (though where he learned that in Massachusetts, I hadn't a clue). He never went anywhere, even the movies, without wearing his broken-in brown cowboy boots, and he carried a bandanna in his pocket instead of a handkerchief.

Francis had an acne-scarred face, but his blue eyes made me wobbly in the knees until I let him kiss me. That kiss left my lips so bruised and raw that I avoided repeating the experience.

"I keep telling Francis that he has to love you less in order for you to love him at all," Mom said, apropos of nothing, over breakfast one morning. "But he just won't listen."

"You talk to Francis about me?" I was horrified in the way only a teenage girl can be by her mother.

She waved her cigarette at me. "Well, what was I supposed to do? He's so desperate," she said, pouring herself a second cup of coffee. "That's not necessarily a bad thing. You always want to be with a man who loves you more than you love him."

Men, in my mother's view, were useful rather than necessary. She relied on Francis for his trailer, to help her take the horses to shows and perform animal rescues. Whenever they heard about animals being neglected or abused, they'd contact the animal control officer and show up with Francis's trailer if the animals had to be removed. Mom would nurse the horses back to health and use them in her riding lessons, or she'd give them to girls whose families would pay the board.

In this way we acquired Sniffles, a Shetland pony that flew into rages if you tried to boss him around. Since Sniffles was so small—his back reached no higher than my waist—Mom decided that the shaggy bay pony would be the ideal candidate to introduce my brother Philip, now five years old, to the joys of horseback riding.

"After all," Mom mused, "he needs something to do, poor kid."

This was a true statement. Philip was just as wild as Donald had been, though he expressed himself intellectually rather than physically. He had started reading as a four-year-old and, with Grandmother to spur him along, was already devouring my father's *Time* magazines every week. Whereas Donald at that age was scaling walls and stealing tips from waitresses, Philip was mouthy and big-headed, correcting his teachers rudely whenever they misspelled something or made a mistake. He had elicited a phone call from the school after taking a hundred-dollar bill from Dad's dresser and presenting it for show-and-tell. During story hour, he had opened his desk lid and slammed it shut to protest the teacher's decision to repeat a certain picture book rather than choose a new one.

My mother's responses to the teacher's complaints were casual. "If she continues to bore Philip in school, then I can't be responsible for the consequences," she sniffed. "You'd think elementary school teachers would wise up and do something different for boys than they do with girls."

So, one bright autumn afternoon, I eagerly saddled up Sniffles. Francis picked Philip up and sat him on the pony's back.

Sniffles ran away immediately, taking the bit in his teeth and snatching the reins out of my little brother's hands. We chased Sniffles all around the riding ring, the pony's eyes rolling as his little hooves churned dirt, until Sniffles found the gate and made a dash for it.

Philip raised his arms and let himself be scraped off the pony's back as Sniffles plunged under the gate and headed straight for the grain room. Philip never rode another horse.

Sniffles proved to be just as feisty when Mom tried to harness him to pull a driving cart a week later. "This pony's eyes turn red whenever I try to get him to do something useful," Mom said in frustration. "I can't control him at all."

"Let me try," Francis suggested.

Mom handed him the driving harness. As he approached Sniffles with the leather straps dangling over one arm, Sniffles reared like the Black Stallion, pawing at the air with his hooves, eyes gleaming. Sure enough, those eyes looked red to me.

Mom and I ducked behind the mounting block in case the pony decided to charge us. But Francis dropped the harness and grabbed both of the pony's front legs. He pushed Sniffles up higher on his back legs, nearly toppling him over backward, and held him that way until the pony's eyes rolled white and the sheer terror of being so unbalanced made his neck foam with sweat.

Gently, Francis let him down. He buckled the harness onto Sniffles's back without further incident and gave the pony a smart smack on his shaggy brown rump. "There now, old boy," Francis murmured. "I wager you won't give these ladies any more trouble, will you? Because you know I'm watching you."

Watching Francis as he danced with that pony and let him down so gently, and surrounded by the sweet autumn scents of hay and oats mixed with molasses, I wished, with all my being, that there could be some way to make yourself fall in love with the man who worked hardest to win your heart.

Chapter Fifteen

A Lady Always Wears Underpants

At the prom

Many years before the gerbils entered our lives, my grandparents owned a gift shop in Bangor, Maine. Mom drove us north from Virginia to stay with them whenever Dad was at sea. The gift shop was a barn where my grandparents sold antiques and pottery, oil paintings small enough to hold in your palm, and china cats curled up on miniature rugs that Grandmother crocheted herself.

Their house was even better. A creaky old white Colonial with broad pine floors and rocking chairs in the kitchen, the house had a view of the river and a generous sun porch. In winter, the snow drifted above the first-floor windows, and in summer wild blueberries grew in the fields around the house. To Donald and my cousins and me, Maine was paradise.

Maine was also where Mom and Grandmother first tried to impress upon me that a lady always wears underpants.

This happened during the summer my cousin Candy was visiting. She was my age and had red hair the color and texture of a rusty scrub pad. One day, after Candy and I had run through the tangle of blueberry bushes below the house, we returned with our legs scratched and bleeding. Our palms and tongues were black from eating as many blueberries as we'd picked. Grandmother sent us straight upstairs to bathe.

We spent a long time in the bubbles. Then we emerged from the bathroom with our towels draped around us like elegant floor-length gowns and paraded around the attic bedroom we shared with Donald, daring my little brother to show us his if we showed him ours.

Grandmother caught us at this game. "You girls put on your underpants *this minute*!" she cried, wringing her hands. "Ladies *always* wear underpants!"

The very next night, Candy and I took another bubble bath after dinner—Lord, how we loved that old claw-footed tub—and came downstairs in our nightgowns with an exciting plan: to show her parents, my parents, our grandparents, and even dumb Donald how we could stand on our heads at the same time, elbow to elbow, a trick we'd been practicing for a week.

We summoned our audience into the living room and directed them to sit while we assumed our pyramid positions, with our heads on the braided wool rug in front of the fireplace and our bony knees propped on our elbows. And then, wobbling but regaining our balance, we slowly raised our legs in the air and pointed our toes like ballerinas. Our nightgowns fell like soft cotton curtains over our heads, and there we stood, upside down and blinded by flannel, the blood rushing to our cheeks as we imagined our toes touching the ceiling.

"Girls, girls, girls!" Grandmother clapped her hands so sharply that we both toppled right over. "You forgot your underpants! Never, *ever* forget your underpants! A lady *always* wears underpants!"

A lady must wear underpants: that was the first rule in

an entire code book that Mom and Grandmother heroically tried to convey to me throughout my adolescence. Other rules included:

A lady always sits with her legs crossed at the ankles. You don't want to show the world your business.

A lady doesn't flounce. She glides.

A lady wouldn't roll her eyes at that.

A lady never calls a boy first.

Ladies do not laugh like hyenas.

A real lady minds her manners at the dinner table.

Ladies always modulate their voices.

A lady would never, ever use that tone of voice with her parents.

A lady knows when to say no.

By the time I started high school in Massachusetts, it was clear that you could not use the words *fun* and *lady* in the same sentence. I was therefore eager to discover what it was like not to be one. This was no simple matter, since so many of the lady rules had something to do with sex, and I couldn't get a boyfriend to stick around long enough to really take that code book for a test drive. As one boy put it, "The only person in the world scarier than your father is your mother."

My first boyfriend was Brian, the brother of Sheri the serial killer. I chose him out of self-preservation. Brian was a thug of a kid with a buzz cut, squinty blue eyes, and the square jaw of a superhero. He sat next to me in Spanish, the only college-bound class on his schedule, and slept through every hour of *¡Hola! ¿Cómo te llamas?* lolling at his desk so that his legs sprawled into the aisle. Other people were so afraid of Brian that they chose other aisles if they needed to sharpen pencils at the back of the room rather than try to step over him. This was fine with me. Whenever his sister and the other girls tried to bully me, Brian bullied them harder.

In the beginning of this relationship, our kisses were chaste and inexperienced. Yet as Brian and I pressed our clothed bodies together, I understood why my mother had been so anxious to drill me on ladylike behavior and keep me out of the clutches of Dad's student merchant Marines in New York: sex was fun!

Every spare minute that first winter I rode my bike down to the Boat Club to meet Brian, who drove across the frozen lake from his house to the Boat Club by snowmobile. The snowmobile was exhilarating and dangerous, the perfect aphrodisiac. I loved straddling the seat behind Brian and pressing my body against his as we fishtailed on the icy lake or plunged through the woods on narrow trails, the tree branches clawing at our helmets. We couldn't talk over the engine noise or the cold rush of wind.

Once we reached our favorite spot, an overgrown Christmas tree farm where the tight rows of tall pines created a secret dell even on snow-bright days, we'd shut off the snowmobile. Deafened by the silence broken only by the steady *drip, drip* of ice melting off the tree boughs, we unzipped our jackets and reached wherever we could with our hands and mouths. Sometimes Brian and I were so absorbed in each other that other snowmobilers surprised us midgrope. We'd have to press our bare torsos together as they roared by, cheering and whistling.

When the ice was gone, Brian could still fetch me from the town beach by boat, racing across the water in his father's inboard to meet me. He always drove in that reckless, immortal way of teenage boys everywhere, the nose of the boat flung high in the air as he gunned the engine.

Mom and Grandmother caught us the day that I told them I was riding my bike to school for exercise and needed to leave an hour early to make it on time. I pedaled down to the Boat Club, where Brian had already tied his boat up at the dock. It was chilly and had rained the night before. Since everything was still damp in the boat, we huddled on the sunny steps of the Boat Club and began kissing.

In anticipation, I'd worn nothing under my jeans and T-shirt. No underpants, no bra. No lady was I!

Brian had just hiked my shirt up when I spotted Mom and Grandmother over his shoulder. They marched toward us in tandem, faces set in grim expressions beneath matching helmets of dark hair. It was like being set upon by zombies.

I stood up, knees trembling, brushed off my jeans, and went to them without a word, praying that they wouldn't notice that I'd left home without my underpants.

"This kind of thing is never going to happen again," Mom said. "This is not the way any daughter of mine is going to behave."

"Or a granddaughter of mine," Grandmother added. "We raised you to be a lady."

"What was I doing that was so wrong?" I wailed. "We were just kissing!"

Mom shook her head. "You were muckled onto that boy like a barnacle on a boat," she said.

I folded my arms against my braless chest, still afraid they'd discover my secret unladylike state. "I don't see what's so wrong with kissing," I insisted.

"Kissing leads to other things," Grandmother sniffed. "It's just like marijuana and heroin. And why should a boy buy the cow when he can get the milk for free?"

We loaded my bike into the station wagon while Brian roared off in his boat across the lake behind us. Brian could bully his sister and her friends; he'd been in knife fights and gotten drunk enough to punch out a kid at a basketball game. He'd even thrown a chair at a kid across the cafeteria. But he was no match for Mom and Grandmother.

"How did you find me?" I asked sullenly as Mom pointed the car toward the high school.

Grandmother rolled her eyes. "We weren't born yesterday, you know."

~

AFTER Brian, I fell in love with a car and went out with the boy who owned it: a souped-up Mustang owned by a senior named Reggie. Reggie had a bowl haircut and was slightly shorter than my own five feet four inches even in his Frye boots, but I overlooked all of this because I loved racing in the Mustang. Reggie would put his car up against Clay Jenson's Corvette along Snow Road and we'd break 110 mph, screaming around the curves and praying there wasn't a hay wagon coming the other way. One night, Clay flipped his Corvette on a patch of black ice and landed upside down in a ditch, but the roll bar kept him and his girlfriend from dying. Clay's car was totaled, but we found other people to race and went on as before.

All of this was so thrilling that I let Reggie take me parking by the river and put my hand on his penis. To my surprise it felt hot and rubbery, not at all what I was expecting. I might have gone further than that, too, but I had a strict curfew and my father, towering over Reggie, had made sure that my new boyfriend knew what it was.

The relationship would have lasted longer if I'd never invited Reggie to dinner at our house. Once Mom met him, she didn't let up, asking me every week when I was going to break up with him.

"What do you care?" I finally asked her furiously. "Reggie's a nice guy. He takes me places. He pays for me at the movies."

"He's too old for you," she said. "Three years makes a lot of difference at your age. And that boy stinks of pig manure."

"He can't help that!" I cried, offended mostly because I'd noticed the stink, too. "His dad's a pig farmer. And anyway, I probably smell like gerbils!"

"Gerbils have no odor," Mom said automatically.

This was a myth perpetuated by my father. It may even have been true for pet gerbils. But given the numbers we had, the gerbil stink could make you cry for mercy. How was it possible, I wondered, that Mom so confidently pegged pigs lower on the farm animal status scale than gerbils? Somehow she did, though, and coming from her it even sounded rational.

I ignored Mom's views on Reggie and invited him home again. Not to dinner, but afterward, when I thought everyone in my family would be safely mesmerized by the television. This time, Reggie brought his guitar and sat with me in the dining room with the swinging doors shut. He proceeded to play "Wild Horses" by the Rolling Stones, gazing deeply into my eyes as he plucked the strings.

"Wild, wild horses, couldn't drag me away-ay!"

I wanted to be awed. Or, at the very least, not horrified. Sadly, though, Reggie was a lamentable musician. He played most of the right chords but sang like someone who'd grown up underwater.

I tried my best to keep a straight face as the ballad dribbled on. Soon it would be over and we could go for a drive in his Mustang.

Then I noticed the swinging door twitching a little behind Reggie. I prayed that it was one of the cats. Or one of the dogs. Or even little Philip. Anyone, dear God, but my brother Donald.

The door swung open a bit more and stayed open. Now I could see Donald lip-synching the words behind Reggie. My brother was clutching his heart and batting his eyelashes at me. Even worse, Mom, Grandmother, Grandfather, and Phil were all crowded in the doorway, too, making faces as my oblivious suitor serenaded me with all his heart.

"Wild, wild horses, couldn't drag me away ay!" Reggie yodeled, and my mother rolled her eyes and then, I swear to God, pinched her nose shut with two fingers.

After that night, I never saw Reggie again.

~

My best friend in West Brookfield was Bea Wilson, whom I met in freshman English class. The class was taught by Mr. Adams, a soulful Peace Corps dropout, the son of a minister who had us singing protest songs and writing short stories full of dark angst. We modeled our stories after his own impenetrable fiction, which Mr. Adams handed out on a regular basis as part of our classroom reading.

Mr. Adams also directed a ninth-grade play about slavery, where I played a black man hoeing fields and singing "Oh, freedom, oh, freedom! Oh, freedom over me!" The intensity of opening night was marred for me only by a gym teacher sitting in the front row. At the sight of me in a black sweater and suspenders, he told his buddy beside him, "They sure didn't build girls like that in my day, no sirree."

Bea's farmhouse stood on a hill on the opposite side of West Brookfield. It was even older and colder than mine. But her house had delightfully sloped ceilings and tilted floors, and the wallpaper was a warm riot of flowers in every room.

Bea's father and mother were both from wealthy families. Her father, JoJo, had worked as an engineer for a large company before deciding to "defect from our money-grubbing imperialist U.S. Government and escape those goddamn whining capitalists," he confided in me one afternoon as he wrapped aluminum foil around their TV antenna to get better reception. In West Brookfield, he declared, "I can be one of the real people living off the land."

On his own 350 acres, JoJo tried pig farming but quit when the barn burned down. He then created a mobile home park and lived off the land that way. "My dad's a good example of how not to work for anybody else," Bea explained. "I guess he's a lot like your dad that way."

This much was true. Most of my friends had fathers who drove sedans or station wagons. These dads came to the high school basketball games and took their families out for Sunday drives. Other than that, they disappeared in the morning and came home at night. None of my friends seemed to know, or care, what their fathers did, whereas Bea and I were privy to every move our fathers made. There was a still a difference between us, however. Bea had little involvement in her father's life, but my brothers and I were enlisted troops serving Dad and his secret mission: raising gerbils to the nth degree. My father, like Bea's dad, worked for himself. But unlike Bea's dad, who seemed to have plenty of free time on his hands, Dad traipsed up to the gerbil building early every morning and didn't return to the kitchen until just before dinner, when he'd pour himself a tall scotch and settle his briefcase on the dining room table. He made his business our business.

In the end, though, none of these comparisons between our fathers was as interesting to me as the fact that Jojo was a nudist. Nobody in that family wore underpants. Bea's jeans had holes that left pink dime-sized circles of skin showing on her butt and thighs. And when Jojo headed out to the frog-choked pond in front of their house to shimmy out of his ragged blue jeans and fling himself onto the grass, his lack of underpants clearly answered any lingering questions I had about what made men different from women.

I had touched Brian's penis, but here was a penis for me to examine in the clear light of day. It was neither alluring nor intimidating. Jojo's penis was simply a wrinkled pink part of him, like the nose on his face.

Besides our rundown houses and our isolationist fathers, the other thing that drew Bea and me together was our shared passion for horses. Her grey gelding even looked like a larger version of Ladybug. I often trotted Ladybug down Long Hill Road, across the town common, and up the hill to Bea's house on weekends, about six miles in all. We'd spend the day riding and the night singing folk songs while Bea played her guitar.

One night, we camped out in the wooden bunkhouse that JoJo had built deep in the woods "in case the tax man ever comes." The bunkhouse was a roughhewn building that required careful maneuvering to avoid catching the wide bell bottoms of our hip-hugger jeans on the nail points sticking out of the clapboards.

"We've made booby traps for ourselves, haven't we?" Bea asked mournfully as I tried to untangle one of her long blond braids from a nail. "We might just as well nail ourselves up on crosses for the tax man to find."

~

ONE summer day between freshman and sophomore year of high school, Bea and I saddled up our horses early and met in the center of town. We rode up one of the farm lanes and played tag in the cornfields, ducking low against the horses' necks to protect our faces from the cornstalks as we raced along the furrows. Afterward, we rode over to the drive-in restaurant on Route 9 and sat astride our sweaty horses between the parked cars, eating ice cream cones and licking the drips off our bare arms.

On the way back, we veered off down the road toward the town beach. It was still early and the beach was nearly empty. We stripped off our saddles and bridles and used the horses' manes to pull ourselves onto their backs. Then we urged the animals into the cool green water with shouts and hard thumps of our heels against their sides until the horses finally charged into the lake, scattering the few swimmers around us.

We rode them deeper into the water until the horses were swimming, too. Ladybug churned the water with her hooves and I floated just above her, legs out straight behind me, clinging to her mane and laughing.

Eventually, one of the swimmers phoned the chief of police to alert him to the beasts in the water. The chief arrived with the siren shrieking atop his cruiser and got out to stand on the beach.

"You girls should know better than to swim those horses here," he shouted. He kept one hammy hand on his gun, but looked overheated and wistful just the same.

We said we were sorry and rode the horses back out onto the beach, feeling the great power of them as the police chief backed away from us. We tacked the horses up again and returned to town, where we let the horses drink at the fountain in the center of the common and thought about what else to do with our Saturday.

The fountain had a sculpture of two seated women in flowing gowns that reached their toes. The statue was pristine white, with just a bit of green mold like lace edging along the edges of the cement dresses. A town vandal with a sense of humor had painted the women's toenails pink.

As the horses slurped and snorted, Bea and I heard music

coming from beyond the stand of tall maples lining the common. It was a man singing, accompanied by a guitar. We trotted the horses over and saw a lanky, freckled redhead sitting with his back against one of the trees, an acoustic guitar in his lap. He gazed up at us on our horses, grinned, and started singing "Lady Godiva":

Seventeen, a beauty queen
She made a ride that raised a scene
In the town . . .

"What other songs do you play?" I asked once he was finished.

"What don't I?" he asked.

"It's true," Bea said, for she'd known this man, Michael, since she was in first grade and he was in sixth with her older brother. He'd been drafted and sent to Vietnam the previous year at age nineteen. Now he was back and living in the caretaker's cottage of the biggest lake house.

We slid down off the horses and drop-tied them next to the tree, where their heads drooped and they swished their tails. The three of us sang protest songs about Vietnam and laughed over all of the words we didn't know. After we tired of this, we followed Michael across the common, leading the patient horses behind us, and went to the Lallys' barn. This was a place I'd heard about but never been invited into. It was a red-shingled pole barn with a sway-backed roof. The Lallys were a family of four brothers and a single mother; the father had died two years earlier of cancer. Two of the Lally boys worked for my father. One of them was in jail now for reasons Dad said I didn't need to know.

The Lally boys had hung music posters and flags on every wall and beam of the barn, along with Indian bedspreads, Christmas lights, and a collection of license plates. There were guitars in the barn, a drum set, and a piano. Teenagers could be found there day or night, sleeping, drinking, getting high, having sex, or just being there because everyone else was.

On this particular morning, half a dozen kids were sleeping on couches that looked as old as the barn, with cotton stuffing spilling out of the cushions. Bea and Michael passed a joint around with the youngest Lally boy, but I refused to smoke. It was too much like what my parents did, and I expected it to make me cough.

Eventually, Bea said she had to go home. She grabbed hold of the pommel of her saddle, hauled herself onto her horse, and dreamily trotted down the middle of Route 9, her yellow braids bouncing against her back, oblivious of the cars honking their horns behind her.

Afterward, Michael took my hand and led me out to the cornfield behind the barn. We found a shady spot at one edge of it beneath an old willow tree. Michael pulled off his T-shirt and spread it on the ground. Without any words at all, I lay down on that T-shirt like it was a magic flying carpet and waited for him to take me somewhere.

Michael was the most beautiful boy in the world, with his red hair and freckles, and skin like peeled new potatoes, white and cool and slick to the touch. His guitarist's fingers did things that made me stop breathing, and then he lay back on his crossed arms beside me in the shade, staring up at the leaves on the old apple tree above us.

When nothing more happened, I sat up and pulled off my shirt. I'd stopped wearing a bra because Bea never wore one, so I thought for sure something unladylike might happen if I was shirtless, too. But Michael shook his head and laughed.

"Get dressed, Lady Godiva," he said.

"Why?" I asked, so mortified that I crossed my arms in front of my chest. "Don't you like me?"

"Of course I do. But you're not old enough to be with me. Don't take things too fast, okay?" He pulled me close for one more kiss. "Promise me that. You're good the way you are. It's the world that's a rotten place."

I didn't understand any of this, but I put my shirt back on and then napped with my head on his shoulder.

As I rode home, trotting Ladybug up Long Hill Road, Michael chunked along behind me in his ancient black Volvo. He helped me put away the horse and tack, and then we sat on the front steps of my house, where Michael played the same melancholy folk songs that he'd strummed on the common. Suddenly Dad appeared, shooting up the driveway in his red Ford station wagon.

Dad must have seen us from the car. He came around the corner of the house at a trot, shouting at Michael to stand up, "and that's an order!"

Michael obeyed instantly, the guitar dangling from one pale hand, and pushed his long hair out of his eyes. He was six feet tall, but next to my father he looked like a chastened twelve-year-old boy, skinny and vulnerable, his Adam's apple bobbing as Dad shouted at him the way I imagined he had done with all of those sailors and soldiers on board his ship or in his classrooms.

"Who are you?" Dad demanded. "And what the hell are you doing here with my daughter?"

Michael mumbled something about just passing the time with a little music, if that was all right.

"It most certainly is not all right," Dad said. "My daughter is fifteen years old, for God's sake, and you're a middle-aged man. I'm asking you to leave the grounds immediately. Do not come back. Do not make me get my Navy pistol."

The pistol, I knew, was a cobwebbed relic hanging above our fireplace. But Michael scrambled to his feet, ran to his Volvo, and tossed the guitar into the backseat through the window.

"You've ruined my life!" I shouted at my father, who was still glaring after Michael's car long after it was out of sight. "He'll never come back now!"

Dad shook his head. "My job is to protect you," he said. "A man that age has no business being here. A man that age is thinking about only one thing with a girl like you."

"You don't *know* that." Stung, I wheeled around and slammed open the screen door against the house. "And anyway, I was thinking about it more than he was," I muttered.

"I hope not. We expect you to act like a lady," Dad said. "Be glad I got here in time to save you from yourself."

Chapter Sixteen

Saving the Blond Gerbil

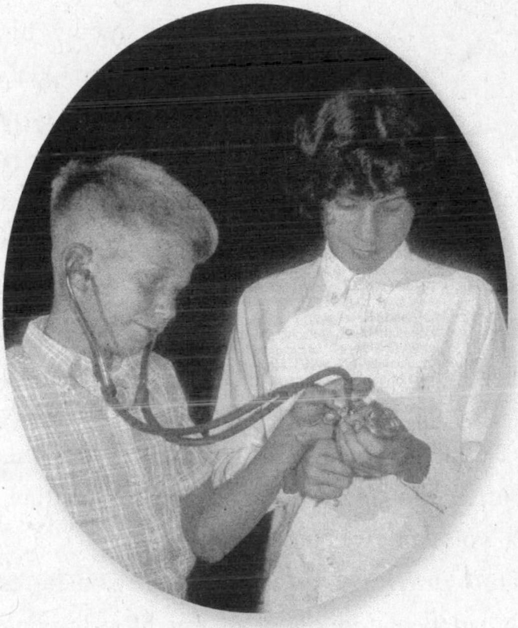

Playing doctor

CREDIT: D. G. ROBINSON JR.

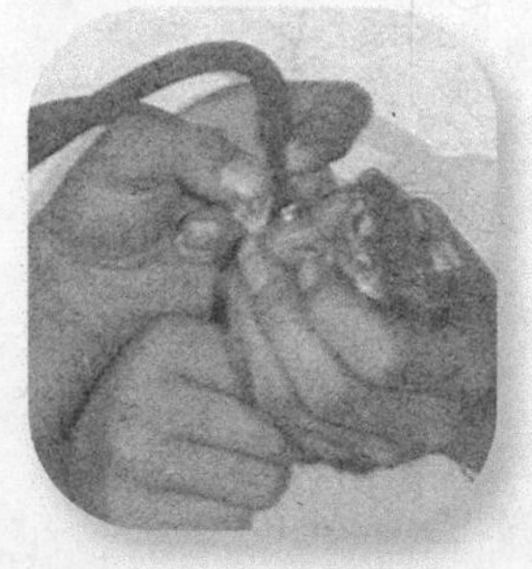

From the start, I was labeled "college-bound" by my high school guidance counselor at Quaboag, who steered me away from typing, wood shop, home economics, art, or any other classes where you actually *did* something. It wasn't until junior year that I finally defied him and signed up for art.

The art teacher was known as "Lamb Chops" for the size and shape of her buttocks and thighs, always encased in skintight jeans beneath bright cotton tops. She was so nonchalant about attendance and behavior that students never missed her class. In fact, there were always extra students hanging around with Lamb Chops; if you wanted to draw, paint, or make pots, you were welcome.

I began to draw with an intensity previously reserved for reading. I had been doodling all my life, drawing animals, mostly, thousands upon thousands of horses and dogs, all of them with noble profiles and muscular necks. Now, Lamb Chops taught me to draw not my imagined ideals but what was really in front of me.

As I studied lines, angles, colors, shadows, and perspectives, I remembered how my own mother used to bring her sketchpad everywhere, or set up her easel and paints in our various family rooms and backyards. I had a distinct memory of hugging Mom and breathing in her special perfume, which I realized only now must have been turpentine.

"Why don't you paint anymore?" I asked Mom one morning as we mucked out stalls. "You used to love it."

"I don't need to paint anymore," she told me. "I just did it because I liked it. Then I got bored and moved on to other things. That's the way I am." She stopped working for a minute and straightened up to lean on the pitchfork. "It's not like you can make a living as an artist, anyway."

"That's not the point of art, to make a living," I said. "It's something you do for your soul."

"Your soul?" Mom laughed. "God. You really are a hopeless romantic." The way Mom said it, "hopeless romantic" was a dire prognosis, like leprosy or leukemia. "You certainly didn't get that from me." She dug her pitchfork into the manure and started shoveling again.

"Well, it can't be from Dad," I said.

"Oh, you'd be surprised," Mom said. "The two of you are more alike than you think."

I pondered this troubling comment the next day as I pedaled my bike downtown to my new job at the Top Hat Diner, a job that mostly involved serving coffee and grilled muffins to old men in duck-billed caps. That I would turn out like my father, whom I saw as methodical and overly focused, stern and unyielding, instead of like Mom, whose charisma attracted people to her like deer to a salt lick, was appalling to me. I didn't want to grow up to be a penny-pinching worrier who thought I would be electrocuted every time I took a shower during a thunderstorm. How could my mother possibly call Dad a romantic?

Though defining what my father *was* posed a problem now that Dad was no longer in the Navy. He wasn't a businessman, store clerk, farmer, or police officer like any of the other fathers I knew. He didn't watch sports on television or drink beer or go fishing. He didn't take my mother out to dinner, other than on her birthday, and he never went to plays or movies. He never read novels. He never had fun.

In fact, I couldn't think of a single thing my father did that wasn't productive. My dad never went anywhere and seemed to have no friends. He scarcely even talked to his own family back in Ohio. The one time his sister and her husband had visited, they'd slept in their camper parked in our yard.

My father's sole identity seemed to be a workaholic whose singular passion in life was to produce more gerbils than anyone else in the world. In the process of applying to colleges, I struggled to come up with a satisfactory answer to scribble into that blank line that cropped up on every application and financial aid form: *Father's occupation.*

On the blank lines, I tried out "retired Navy officer," "scientist," "author," and, in a daring creative stroke, "livestock breeder." I had grown up hiding what my father did. I wasn't about to change now.

At the same time, it seemed wrong not to mention gerbils. No matter how I felt about them, or about what Dad did with them, gerbils were going to put me through college. They deserved some credit, I thought.

Finally, I settled on this benign phrase: "gentleman farmer." And for my academic major, I wrote, "very undecided."

~

THE upside of Dad being such a single-minded workaholic was that his business grew steadily every year. Each month brought more gerbil orders than the last, thanks to ads in laboratory animal magazines, Dad's personal appearances at laboratory animal conferences, and his recent and most successful marketing tool by far: a quarterly newsletter he dubbed the *Gerbil Digest*.

As with his letterhead, the *Digest* logo was a small house on the cover with "Home of the Gerbil" written in Chinese characters below the roof. The *Digest* also featured one of Dad's photographs, a black-and-white portrait of a gerbil nibbling on a seed.

The point of this newsletter was to ratchet up the cycle of gerbil supply and demand. For each issue, Dad spent hours, even days, at the University of Massachusetts library in Amherst, where he was now taking graduate courses in zoology, to read the most recent scholarly articles about ongoing gerbil research—most of it done with his own animals.

He summarized the research into a newsletter format, made dozens of copies, and paid Donald, Philip, and me to collate and staple the pages, a job I loathed because it required walking around the dining room table until I was dizzy and avoiding staple gun fights with Donald. Dad's careful market research and our stapling efforts paid off, though: the *Gerbil Digest* was soon recognized as such a valuable biomedical research tool that it was indexed in *Biological Abstracts*.

In this fashion, Dad made gerbils increasingly indispensable to the world. By my junior year of high school we were housing over six thousand gerbils. Our second building was filled to capacity. We had an emergency generator to maintain power in the gerbil buildings because they had to be climate-controlled, and Dad listed over a dozen employees on the payroll in addition to family members. He was now contemplating the construction of a third building over Mom's protests.

With all of this action in our back pastures, people in town couldn't help but finally notice that something was up. That winter, the trees all seemed to shed their leaves during the same week when Massachusetts was walloped with the first snowstorm of the season. As a result, our twin gerbil buildings were suddenly revealed like a pair of gleaming metal cruise ships grounded on an iceberg.

This arresting sight caused a pair of townie kids to circle my locker at school the next morning. The boys had greasy hair down to their shoulders, pot breath, and clunky Frye boots that ripped the muddy hems of their bell-bottoms.

"Hey, Holly," one of them drawled, imitating my Virginia accent, "how y'all doin' up there yonder at the rat farm?"

"Yeah," his friend snorted. "What's Commander Mouse up to these days?"

The two of them followed me down the hall, cackling like hyenas. "What are you doing after school, rat farmer's daughter? Want to get high?"

After school, I stormed straight off the bus and out to the stable, where Mom was tacking up horses for lessons. "The kids at school are calling Dad a rat farmer. I *hate* it that people think we're nuts!" I complained.

Mom didn't even bother to turn around. "What do you care what those stupid kids say?" she asked. "You know that we're better than they are. Let them think what they want. They will, anyway. Just ignore them."

That was the thing about Mom. No matter what happened, she knew that she was better than anyone else. Meanwhile, I was constantly on alert, hiding whatever freakish tendencies I had toward reading, science, and horses to avoid ridicule.

I said nothing as rumors spread through school about rats and mice on Tumblebrook Farm. This grew more difficult as accusations flew: My father was an evil scientist who boiled rats for supper. He sold mice for fur. He had deals to send his mice into space. (This part was nearly true: Dad had been in discussion with NASA about sending his gerbils into space, but mice won out because of better genetic mapping.)

I bit my tongue through it all. Dad never did anything to correct the impression that people in town had of us as rat farmers, either. In fact, whenever I complained at home about these rumors, he actually looked pleased. Dad's theory was that animal activists were far less likely to bother camping out on our fields if they thought we were only raising rats.

"Most people think mice and rats are 'ew,' " he explained. "They really don't care much about what happens to them. Gerbils are a different kettle of fish. It's the pet thing." He wagged a finger at me. "Remember, Holly. Nobody needs to know our business but us."

~

NO MATTER how many hours a week I worked for my father or how much I resented the weirdness of his business, I never got tired of the gerbil pups. Scarcely an inch long, the newborn gerbils were deaf and toothless, as blind as kittens, and as naked as lizards. Within a week, though, they blinked at the world around them, sprouted brown mossy fuzz, and cheeped like chicks. At three weeks, they hopped about in their cages, big-eyed miniatures of the adults.

Cleaning cages meant having to destroy their nests. After seeing how frantic the families became, I defied my father's orders to empty every bit of soiled litter. Instead, I saved small handfuls of the original nesting material to add to the clean cages before dropping the gerbil families into their new homes. I justified this secret rebellion by reasoning that having something familiar to smell and sleep in would lower gerbil stress and make for happier, healthier gerbil families.

I felt loyal to the gerbils partly because I was so impressed by gerbil family life. If separated from their mates, gerbils are so loyal that they often refuse to take another one. Another big plus is that they hardly ever gobble down their young.

Gerbils are also great communicators. They make good use of their long back feet, thumping them to warn of danger or wow potential mates. If a gerbil rolls onto its back in front of another gerbil, it wants a grooming session. If one gerbil becomes annoyed with another, it simply butts the pest away without doing serious harm.

All in all, gerbils did a better job of getting along than most people, I thought, watching my own parents spar. Mom was more verbal and usually won their arguments, which almost always focused on money. She routinely stormed off during their "conversations," usually after tossing a grenade of a one-liner. Afterward, Dad would stare into space through a haze of cigarette smoke or, more dramatically, sigh with his head in his hands.

And, like gerbils, Mom would butt Dad away physically, using her shoulder or hip whenever he tried to wrap his arms around her waist at the kitchen sink or put his arm around her on the couch.

"How come you never kiss Dad?" I dared to ask Mom once.

She shrugged. "It's hardly necessary when you're married," she said. "Being married is just like being in business together, only you don't ever get to take a vacation."

I thought about my feverish kisses with Brian, Michael, and the other boys I'd dated—all of them briefly. Thanks to my family, I probably wouldn't ever meet someone who stuck around long enough for me to marry. But that was okay, I decided. Judging by my parents, marriage seemed like a pesky but nonfatal condition, like a chronic cold or a bad back. Some days were better than others, but mostly you just had to survive marriage one day at a time.

DURING many of our family dinners, Dad casually reported on the journeys of our gerbils as if they were cousins or friends taking vacations. "I sent three dozen breeding pairs to Ann Arbor, Michigan, today," he might begin, or "Dr. Wong called to say that our fifty weanlings arrived in Miami on time despite that thunderstorm." But we never talked about what actually happened to the gerbils once they arrived at their final destinations, despite the fact that Donald and I helped Dad ship his gerbils around the world.

The animals usually traveled by jet in cardboard boxes lined with wire mesh. These boxes came in flats that Donald and I helped Dad assemble as needed. We also metered out food pellets and carrot stubs, which provided a water supply for gerbils on the go. We rationed these green and orange tokens according to how many gerbils were in a box and how far they had to travel.

Twice a week, Dad or one of his employees drove to Bradley International Airport with boxes of gerbils stacked in the back of the station wagon, or, if there were too many boxes to fit inside the car, in the rattling Honey Wagon. On the way to the airport there was an obligatory stopover at the local veterinarian's office, where the gerbils were given the once-over and the vet signed a bill of good health, allowing the gerbils to travel.

Even with all of these precautions, occasionally something went awry. Once, for instance, a group of rowdy young gerbils confined to the hold of a Japanese Airlines jet chewed their way out of a shipping box and made a mad dash for freedom. Dad had to consult with the Japanese for several hours, shouting instructions to Japanese technicians over our kitchen phone as he talked them through various strategies for capturing renegade rodents. The Japanese jet had to be grounded for forty-eight hours during this gerbil round-up, for fear that any loose gerbils might chew through the electrical wires while the jet was airborne.

~

ONE night, I lay in bed and contemplated my latest artwork, an aggressive sunset in burnt oranges, murky purples, and hysterical reds that I'd painted over the pale blue Colonial floral wallpaper Mom had so painstakingly hung in my room the month before, causing her to yell at me in a way she usually reserved for Donald. I didn't care, though. I thought my room looked just like an album cover.

Donald poked his head through the doorway and interrupted my reverie. He was taller than I was, now that I was sixteen and he was thirteen, and he'd grown his hair long. His wavy hair was the color of dirt and so thick and tangled that it looked like a preschool art project. Beneath that mop, his eyes were the feverish bright blue of a religious charismatic's.

"What's up?" I asked.

Donald cast a quick look over his shoulder, then poked his head further in. "I saw Dad do it today," he whispered.

"Stay out of my room," I said automatically. "Do what?"

"Kill the extras." Donald's voice was hushed.

"What are you talking about?"

"The extra gerbils! Dad kills them himself, you know. He gasses them. Just like the Nazis with the Jews."

"He does not either! Get out of my room," I said, but without conviction. I had never before allowed myself to wonder what Dad did with surplus gerbils. The reason was simple: on some level pricking below my conscious mind, I knew.

"Dad's got his own personal gas chamber," Donald went on, excited to have my full attention. "It's this big plastic thing that looks like a hatbox. He puts a hose in it and pumps in carbon monoxide from a tank."

"Go *away*!" I threw a book at him. "You're *disgusting*!"

Donald grinned, satisfied. "Mom says quit pretending that

you can't hear her and go downstairs to set the table. Dinner's almost ready."

I laid silverware around the table like a robot. We were having lasagna, one of my favorites, but I couldn't eat. Finally, halfway through dinner, I said, "Dad, tell me the truth. Are you committing gerbil genocide?"

Dad's bald scalp immediately flushed scarlet inside his monk's fringe of gray hair. "Goddamn it, Donald, I told you not to say anything to your sister," he said, and lifted a huge wedge of lasagna to his mouth.

I recognized this tactic: we weren't allowed to speak with our mouths full, so Dad was silencing himself by chewing.

"Holly and I are employees, Dad," Donald reminded him solemnly. "We attend company meetings. We deserve to be in the know."

Dad sighed and continued chewing, but we waited him out. Finally, he put down his fork. "Look, it's like any business. If you have extra inventory, you have to unload it."

"Unload it!" I cried. "These are lives we're talking about!"

"These are gerbils," Dad said patiently. "Rodents. They wouldn't even exist if I weren't breeding them. Their sole purpose is to serve the cause of medical research. If I didn't kill the extra animals, if I had to feed every gerbil that was defective or unsold, I'd go broke. It's a simple matter of doing the math."

"But you're killing innocent animals!" I pushed my plate away. "You're a *murderer*!"

My mother stifled a snigger at the end of the table, and little Philip looked worriedly around at all of us. "Who is Dad killing?" he asked.

"No one," Dad said. "Eat your dinner."

"Anyone need seconds?" Mom said. "It's good lasagna tonight. Going once? Twice? Any takers? No?"

Dad pointed at my plate. "What are you eating, Holly?"

"Lasagna," I said, confused by the sudden shift in topic.

"And what's in lasagna sauce?"

"I don't know. Tomatoes? Onions? Hamburger?"

"And where does hamburger come from?" Dad took another mouthful.

"But that's different," I protested weakly, sick to my stomach. "We don't actually raise our own cows and kill them."

"No. Though perhaps that would be more ethical than letting somebody else do our dirty work," Dad countered. "You don't know how these cows were treated before they died."

"It would be cool to kill our own," Donald said.

"Shut up," I said. "Anyway, I've been thinking about being a vegetarian," I lied. Cheeseburgers were a staple in my diet.

"You'll get anemia," Mom said, waving a hand at this nonsense. "A girl your age needs plenty of iron."

"Because you get *periods,*" Donald said.

Mom gave him a look. "I get periods," she said.

Donald was silenced. The rest of us were, too. Nobody wanted to think about Mom's periods.

"Look," Dad said after a moment. "I don't like killing the gerbils, either, but it's painless. They just go to sleep. It's very humane."

"Like a Nazi gas chamber," Donald said. "The Jews went to sleep, too."

"Jesus Christ, Donald," Dad said.

Mom glared. "I won't have that language at my table."

Donald ignored her. "Sometimes the gerbils don't die right away, you know," he told Dad.

"What?" Dad grabbed a piece of garlic bread and frantically bit into it.

"I've seen it," Donald went on. "Sometimes, if you don't gas them for long enough, the gerbils wake up in the Dumpster and try to escape. They're probably living in our pasture right now."

"They'd never make it through the winter," Mom pointed out.

"Look," Dad said, exasperated. "There's no perfect way to get rid of surplus stock. I sell what I can to pet distributors, but the reality is that production and customer orders are both unpredictable. Plus, researchers often want males instead of females, because they don't want hormones interfering with their studies."

"You mean you kill off mostly *girl gerbils*?" I was nearly hysterical. I'd been reading Sylvia Plath's poetry; now I stood up and recited a line from my favorite poem, "Daddy":

> *Every woman adores a Fascist,*
> *The boot in the face, the brute*
> *Brute heart of a brute like you.*

There was a small silence. Then Mom said, "Good Lord. I certainly hope that's not what they're teaching you at the high school." She stood up and began clearing the table. "Help me get these plates into the dishwasher."

I began clearing the table, but paused in the doorway between the dining room and kitchen. "How can you raise gerbils just to be tortured?" I asked tearfully.

Dad sighed. "They're not tortured," he said. "Scientists are very humane. And this is the only way to make progress in medicine. Without animal research, we might never prevent or cure many potentially fatal diseases. Did you ever stop and think about that?"

We looked at each other for a long moment, but neither of us dared to say Gail's name.

~

AS COLLEGE loomed, Dad earnestly advised me about academic majors. He encouraged me to join ranks with him in the booming gerbil industry. "You're the only one in this family besides me who even likes gerbils," he pointed out. "If you don't take over my business, I don't know who will."

"I don't think so, Dad," I said. "I want to be an artist or a doctor. Or maybe a lawyer." *Anything but a gerbil farmer,* I thought, but couldn't bring myself to say it.

My father shook his head. "You can't be a lawyer. Every time you got your period, you'd cry in front of the judge."

"Chauvinist," I said, but I was afraid that he might be right. I'd always been the soft-hearted one in the family, weeping with the abandon of a menopausal widow whenever there was an injured bird in the yard or a tearjerker TV show. When I was younger, I used to crawl into a prone position beneath the coffee table so that nobody would see me cry.

Inevitably, though, Dad would notice. "Holly's leaving us now," he'd announce. "Good-bye, Holly!"

"Good-bye, Holly!" Mom would echo, calling to me as if she were standing across a crowded train platform.

Despite coexisting with my mother, who regularly trounced him verbally, showed more business savvy, didn't flinch at blood, and tore down walls with crowbars, Dad continued to perceive men as strong leaders and women as vulnerable helpmates. His latest book laid these beliefs out on the page for the whole world to see.

During the two years that Dad was holed up in his bachelor's quarters at the Merchant Marine Academy, he hadn't been content to just teach during the week and get his business started on weekends. He had also approached the Pet Library, the publishing division of Hartz Mountain pet supplies, to ask if they'd like a book about gerbils. They'd immediately given him a contract.

For his new book, *Know Your Gerbils* (1972), Dad recycled some of the information about keeping pet gerbils from his first book and used a few of the same photographs. He also included more recent pictures, the result of various photography sessions at the farm. In these, Donald appeared as a genius scientist or medical professional. Clipboard in hand, my brother looked as if he were meticulously recording the weights of gerbil pups on a scale, charting a gerbil's movements in the mysteriously labeled "open field" test, or sagely cataloging a gerbil's performance on an elevated "Y-maze" track.

I, meanwhile, was relegated in every picture to the role of secretary or nurse. In my only solo appearance, I was dangling a pair of gerbils by their tails, gerbilly asses pointed toward the camera.

It was an unfortunate portrait: Dad caught me looking cross-eyed down my nose to determine, as his caption handily explained, the difference between male and female gerbils by assessing "the animal with the greatest and the one with the least distance between the anal and genital openings."

~

SHORTLY after the publication of *Know Your Gerbils,* Dad's most loyal employee, Angeline, began bemoaning the fate of white gerbils. These were born occasionally as a result of recessive genes; since Dad couldn't sell them with the others—he was still working on producing a pure agouti strain of inbreds prone to seizures—he disposed of them in his hatbox gas chamber.

"Maybe we don't have to let Dad see them," I said.

"How are you going to do that?" Angeline raised one penciled eyebrow under her blond bangs. "We can't hide them forever." She sighed. "I just wish I could take them home. I'd like to breed white gerbils."

"Why don't you?" I asked. "You could save them!"

So, whenever a white gerbil was born, Angeline would wait until it was old enough to wean and then take it home in a cage she kept on the backseat of her car.

"You really don't think I'm stealing?" she asked me anxiously one day, running a hand through her hair as she showed me another white gerbil in a litter of three brown brothers and sisters.

"No. Dad's just going to gas it anyway," I reassured her.

That very afternoon, as if to prove my point, Dad found

a white gerbil that had escaped our notice. He carried the weanling by its tail over to Angeline. "Here's another defect," he said, and handed it to her.

Angeline plucked the gerbil out of Dad's fingers and cradled it between her palms. I didn't dare meet her gaze. "Yes, sir," she said, and carried the gerbil into the room with the gas chamber. I kept Dad talking so that he wouldn't hear her disappear through the side door and out to her car.

Every now and then, I'd find a favorite gerbil and save it, too. I couldn't bring gerbils into our house, but I began hiding them from Dad. The most remarkable of these was a male with a stunning shock of soft blond hair growing right between his ears.

"Look!" I said, showing him to Angeline. "A blond gerbil! Can we save him?"

She grinned and nodded. Angeline and I managed to move the blond gerbil from rack to rack, from room to room, between the gerbil buildings. It was a small, mutinous gesture that my father never noticed at all. But it was something.

Chapter Seventeen

Rebellions

Mom and Philip in the kitchen

CREDIT: THE HOLLY ROBINSON COLLECTION

One night, Dad called a company meeting and summarized the state of affairs at Tumblebrook Farm, reading from an agenda printed on blue paper.

I recognized the paper as the recycled backside of a page from one of the latest issues of the *Gerbil Digest*. Dad's office, along with our basement, attic, and family room floor, was stacked thigh-high with these papers, along with anything else that might come in handy: old *Time* magazines, empty mayonnaise jars of screws, bits of old crown molding, cardboard boxes filled with glass shards, heaps of rags, and emptied cans with the labels removed. Each time Dad used an item from this collection he would sigh with satisfaction and remind us of how we might have thrown it out if not for him.

"At this point in time," Dad announced, his blue eyes lingering on each of us in a sales technique he'd learned by reading a marketing textbook purchased at a yard sale, "Tumblebrook Farm has left its competition behind and continues to produce more gerbils than anyone else in the world. We're charging fixed prices with absolutely no discounts, and I have set gerbil prices as high as the market will bear. Orders are ranging in size from 2 to 450 animals, with the average being between 25 and 100 animals per order. Customers continue to pay for boxes and shipping charges to keep our overhead as low as possible."

"That's good, Dad, right?" I asked.

He nodded and lowered the paper to the table. "I am also pleased to add that company morale is at an all-time high."

Mom lit a cigarette. "We're going to miss *60 Minutes* if we don't wrap this up soon," she reminded him.

"This is important, Sally." Dad picked up his agenda again and pointed at the last two bullet points. "We have reached a critical juncture at Tumblebrook Farm," he went on.

"A what, Dad?" Donald asked. He was bouncing a baseball under the table. Baseballs don't bounce, but that didn't stop him from trying.

My father ignored him and continued reading over the noise. "I am pleased to report that we have a diverse customer list and reasonable expectations of steady growth as the species continues to gain broader acceptance as a test animal. However, we don't want to limit our viability in the future."

"Our what, Dad?" Philip asked. He was using one of the cloth napkins to play tug-of-war with the dogs under the table.

"He doesn't want to put all of his eggs in one basket," I translated.

Dad nodded. "I have therefore decided that this is an appropriate time to add a new species to Tumblebrook Farm, and I'd like to put that to a company vote."

"Not lizards," Mom said. "Please, for the love of God. Not lizards."

"I know. Snakes!" Donald yelped. "Let's breed boa constrictors!"

My father had remarkable powers of concentration. He continued as if nobody had spoken at all. "I was considering chinchillas," he mused. "And I certainly haven't ruled out the colonization of tree shrews and degus, as these animals seem to be gaining in popularity among researchers. However, given our current facilities and manpower, I have decided that African pygmy goats would be the best possible addition to Tumblebrook Farm in the short term."

"Oh, sure, great idea," Mom said. She stood up to clear away the coffee cups. "That way, I get to take care of them at the barn. Am I right? Admit it. That's what's going through your devious little mind."

"Sally, please sit down. I'm not finished here," Dad said.

"Send me a memo," Mom snapped. "*60 Minutes* has already started. Better yet, how about a show of hands, kids? Who votes for an early adjournment, with the discussion to be continued at some future date, after I have a private word with your father?"

Dad was the only one who didn't raise his hand.

~

MY FATHER'S herd of African pygmy goats consisted of eight does and a buck. Not one of them stood higher than my kneecaps. The does were black and white, with sweet tufted beards and gentle dispositions. But the buck had a devil's horns and protruding gold eyes with slit black pupils. He patrolled the yard with a drunk's confident swagger and had a signature stink, like a roadkill muskrat three days old.

Grandfather built a shed for the goats behind the horse stable. We penned them in at night to keep them safe from coyotes, but the pygmy goats were free to graze the farmyard during the day. The little does were easily spooked by our dogs; they'd bleat in distress and bolt into the pasture if the dogs started barking at them. We'd spend hours beating back the tall weeds in the pasture until we found the witless, stubby-legged creatures and led them back. Dad took no part in any of this. Whenever Mom complained about the goats, he'd remind her that the gerbils were "more than full-time, Sally, since I'm chief cook and bottle washer. Get the kids to help you."

About six months after the goats arrived, one of the does was bitten by the buck during a romantic tryst. This love bite caused an abscess in her neck that swelled to the size of a Georgia peach. I cradled the goat in my arms while Mom expertly lanced the lump with a needle. We drained the pus into an empty coffee can until the wound ran clear, and kept the doe in a playpen in our kitchen for several days until she healed completely.

When she seemed frisky again, I carried the doe back to the barn to reunite her with her sisters. She never made it. Along the way, the dogs jumped up at the goat in my arms, barking furiously, and gave her a heart attack. The goat gasped and died, her head lolling back over my arm.

The prancing little buck met an even worse end. Mom and I went up to the barn one morning to feed the horses and discovered that he had hung himself in a bucket. He'd tried to take a drink by putting his head through the bucket handle and broke his own neck while twisting to get free.

"I'm sure it was intentional," Mom said, surveying the

death scene with a sigh. "In any case, that's it for me. I'm done with goats. You can tell your father that for me at the next company meeting."

"Can I have the buck's body, Mom?" Donald asked.

Mom waved a distracted hand. "Just get it out of here," she said. "It's stinking up the stable."

Donald carried the buck out of the barn, and I watched him hike across the street to the old dry well and drop the goat into it.

A few months later, Donald attached a hook to a rope and lowered it down the well to fish out the goat's skeleton. He sawed the skull off and brought it back to his bedroom, where he put it on his bureau with a couple of Ping-Pong balls painted bright green and glued into the eye sockets.

~

REBELLIONS became increasingly commonplace on our farm after that, beginning with my own brothers. Now fifteen, Donald had gotten himself a girlfriend, a bona fide hippie with waist-length blond hair, a wispy voice, Indian-print skirts, unshaved legs, and a passion for creating her own costumes. Her best effort was a gauzy yellow skirt and top that she'd accessorized by punching holes into pennies and sewing them onto the fabric. She shimmied around our yard in that getup at one of my brother's parties, clinking and clanking, belly button winking, until Mom made her come inside and have a cup of coffee. Donald began sneaking out of the house every night to pay her a visit, stealing my parents' car to drive the five miles despite the fact that he was a year short of a driver's license.

Occasionally, Donald rebelled against farm chores, too. Once, as he was lying beneath one of the old Triumph roadsters he was always fixing up, Dad asked him to empty the manure cart out at the stables.

Donald told him to go empty the cart himself. "Or have Holly do it," he suggested. "She's the horse nut."

"That's no job for a lady," Dad reminded him.

"Well, those horses weren't my idea," Donald said. "I wasn't born to shovel shit."

"I don't care. I asked you to do something. Now stop whatever dumb thing you're doing and give me some help," Dad demanded.

Donald hammered at a pipe beneath his car without bothering to answer.

"And that's an order!" Dad growled.

The more Dad tried to order him around, the more Donald ignored him, goading my father until he finally threatened to punish him. "I'll take the belt to you," Dad said. "See if I don't."

"Oh, yeah?" Donald slid out from under the car and stood up, nearly as tall as my father. "You can't punish me if you can't catch me, old man. And we both know you can't catch me anymore."

With that, the race was on. Dad chased Donald around and around the house. Mom heard the commotion and brought out a pitcher of lemonade and some glasses. She and I parked ourselves on the shady patio to watch my father and brother do laps around the farmhouse. Each time he came around to our side of the house, Donald grinned and waved, then disappeared again just as Dad rounded the corner.

After a few minutes of this, Dad was gasping for breath and nearly limping. "I need a cigarette," he complained.

"Here. Have one of mine. Why don't you sit down?" Mom said, and coaxed him onto the patio for a calming smoke and a cold glass of lemonade.

Donald went back to his car. But after a few minutes, he joined us on the patio, too. "All that running made me sweat," he complained. "Now I'm thirsty."

Dad shook his head. "Maybe you should join the Navy," he suggested, while Mom poured out another glass of lemonade. "The Navy will show you how to sweat for real. You should go to Annapolis and have some respect drummed into you."

Donald scoffed at this idea. "Why would I want to get up at five in the morning and do push-ups?"

"Well, then you'll have to take over the gerbils."

"God, no," Donald said. "I'd rather join the Navy."

Dad looked at me. "I don't suppose you've changed your mind?"

"No, Dad. Sorry. It'll have to be Phil," I told him.

Dad sighed. "I'll be dead by then."

It was true that Phil was still little. But even at six years old, he was having a few rebellions of his own. He was especially frustrated in school, where he told us that the other children were stupid, "like three grades dumber than me." Later, an IQ test proved that he was most likely right.

One day, Mom went to pick Phil up early from the elementary school and discovered that the teacher had tucked my little brother into the basement therapy room with other "special" students after he'd corrected her once too often on her spelling. Phil was finally happy, sewing together leather wallets and comb cases, but Mom yanked him out of that school and sent him on to St. Mary's Catholic School in nearby Ware, a mill town best known for its motto, "The town that can't be licked."

"Let's hope the nuns knock some sense into that kid," she said. "If nothing else, he'll learn how to pray."

The animals, meanwhile, were also raising Cain. In retaliation for the goats, Mom had gone against Dad's wishes and brought home several pairs of exotic birds. The first to inhabit our stable yard were two pairs of peacocks. This was a mistake. The peacocks had brain-numbingly beautiful feathers but regularly issued cries as earsplitting as the air horns on semi trucks. Mom also bought Chinese golden pheasants and guinea hens; the pheasants were pleasing to have around, like plumes of sunlight beneath the hedges. But the chubby, black-speckled guinea hens terrorized the dogs and children around the barn by darting out at them from unexpected places. After each attack, the birds cackled and regrouped under the bushes again, huddling in wait for their next victim.

Grandfather had always wanted geese, so he installed half a dozen gray and white geese on the small pond beside the driveway. Grandfather built a little A-frame house for them, complete with fancy gingerbread trim. It looked like a shrunken Swiss chalet. In summer, the goslings sometimes kept my little brother Phil company, leaving their weedy pond to paddle about with my brother in his wading pool.

Occasionally, we lost a gosling to a snapping turtle. One

minute, it would be happily trailing after its mother in the pond. The next, there was nothing but rings of water where the gosling had been dragged under.

But most of the geese lived long, noisy lives, and they were a menace. Whenever someone parked in the driveway and tried to emerge from the car, the geese gave chase, running neck first, beaks open wide to hiss and show their red snake tongues. We kept a broom by the sundeck in case we needed to beat them off.

Mom loved sheep, so these were our next acquisition. "Why not sell wool?" she asked Dad one night at dinner. "How hard could that be? All we'd have to do is let them eat what's already here and shear them once a year."

For once, the entire family was in agreement, envisioning a field of fluffy white lambs cavorting in purple clover beside their even fluffier, money-making mothers. What none of us had anticipated was the overwhelming stupidity of sheep.

We installed a flock of ewes with one ram, white with black ears, and were thrilled to see them grazing in the side yard next to the geese, where handy Grandfather promptly built a sheep shed and a fence. However, the sheep proved to be impossible to contain. They constantly tried to escape through the fence, and we spent hours untangling them from the barbed wire.

The lambs were born in the spring, and this was fun, except for the bit where we had to wrap rubber bands around their tails to cut off the circulation and make the tails fall off. This tactic was meant to keep the wool around their hind ends cleaner, but not one of us had ever imagined the tedium of having to clean up lamb tail stubs that lay like fat cigarettes all around the sheep pen.

One depressed ewe refused to care for her twin lambs at all. We brought the wobbly newborns into the kitchen and kept them in a cardboard box lined with towels next to the kitchen table. The lambs were cute, but the novelty of having to bottle-feed them every two hours finally pushed us over the edge. We sold the entire flock of sheep at an auction scarcely a year after buying them.

"Nobody wears wool anymore, anyway," Mom sniffed as we helped her lead the sheep out to the truck that came to collect them. "It's all about polyester these days."

~

GRADUALLY we added more pets to our household. We still had Beau, the black poodle we'd brought from Kansas, and Yankee, our collie/shepherd mix, who my grandparents had kept in Virginia and brought with them to Massachusetts. We rapidly added more dogs until we had a motley pack. Mom picked up Chrissy, a grinning shepherd mix, from a nearby dairy farm, and Donald brought home Sassy, a miniature Yorkshire terrier puppy small enough to tuck into the pocket of his jacket.

However, Mom still wasn't satisfied. One day she went out on a long drive by herself with no explanation. She came home with a dog from the pound, a shaggy-haired Russian wolfhound. The dog was cream-colored and pointy-nosed; from some angles it looked noble. From others, it looked like a collie that had been run over by a truck. Mom named him Yuri.

Yuri had a temper. Twice, the wolfhound bit visitors to our farm, and he would have happily tasted more if Mom hadn't kept him chained to a post by the back door, from which he lunged at anyone who passed and snapped his long, skinny jaws like a crocodile.

At about the same time, Mom also developed a passion for parrots. We didn't have the money to buy one, so she got a yellow-headed Amazon in the same way we acquired most of our animals: for free, from someone who'd gotten tired of taking care of it. Mom named the parrot Max and kept him in a cage next to the kitchen table, where she fed him bits of bacon and egg every morning from her own plate.

Max and Yuri had twin dispositions. You could only handle Max wearing a thick work glove, and passing Max's cage required a quick dip of the shoulder to avoid being bitten.

All in all, between the guinea hens, the geese, the wolfhound, and the parrot, entering our house became a real challenge. Some people might have thought we didn't want visitors at all.

Chapter Eighteen

What a Gerbil Farmer Does for Fun

Grandmother and Dad

CREDIT: THE HOLLY ROBINSON COLLECTION

Our second summer on Tumblebrook Farm, Dad spent an entire month painting our square house on the hill a deep dirt brown. With so many outbuildings crowded around it, our poor farm now looked like a dark lord's castle surrounded by a feudal village.

To this scene my parents added a swimming pool the summer before my senior year of high school. Gerbils paid for that shimmering blue rectangle, which Dad centered smack in the middle of our property between his metal buildings gleaming in the distance and Mom's stable. My parents spent their summer days tending to their respective animals. Then they retired poolside each evening for cocktails, cigarettes, and summit meetings on neutral turf.

Other than these evening powwows, Dad rarely approached the pool. He did buy himself a new bathing suit, though, a brown bikini Speedo that matched the house paint and emphasized his heron's legs and farmer's tan. I saw him swim maybe twice during my entire adolescence, but he wore that bikini whenever weather permitted. Dad mounted the tractor to mow the lawn in that bathing suit. He washed the car in it. He sawed wood in his Speedo, setting up his table and chain saw close enough to the pool so that flying chips of wood dotted the water's surface like dead beetles. Dad even put his Speedo on to heave gerbil boxes into the back of the station wagon.

"I wish to God you'd put some clothes on," Mom scolded Dad at one point. "You look like a French Canadian tourist in that thing."

"Really, it's the most comfortable article of clothing I own," Dad said. "I'd wear this everywhere if I could."

One hot July day, Dad donned his new Speedo and asked me to help him carry his thermal rods. Thermal rods were my father's newest obsession and business brainstorm; these were six-foot-long black plastic pipes, six inches in diameter and filled with salt crystals.

"You can install these rods anywhere inside the wall of a building," Dad told me that afternoon as I helped him ferry a stack of rods from the enormous truckload dumped next to the driveway over to a pile by the riding arena.

"How do they work?" I asked.

"When the sun hits the wall, the salt substance absorbs heat and turns liquid, dispersing the heat into tubes," Dad said. "At night, when the sun goes down, the heat is exchanged into the room as the salt inside the rods solidifies."

"So you actually own all of these rods?" I asked, eyeing the towering pile of them. Those rods were longer than I was, and as shiny and black as giant licorice sticks.

"Of course." Dad picked up a dozen thermal rods and balanced them across his shoulders. "But only temporarily." He began walking, in his Speedo and sneakers, toward the riding arena, hunched under the load of rods like an ox beneath a yoke. "I'm an agent for the company that manufactures them."

I picked up some of the rods and laid them across my shoulders, as Dad had done, and followed him toward the arena. Dad paused by the garden and spun slowly around to look at me. The rods turned with him. "I can sell thermal rods to anybody who wants them," he announced confidently. "I expect them to fly out of here. There's an energy crisis, you know. People won't be able to get enough of these."

With that, Dad was on his way again, slowly maneuvering the rods on his shoulders along the narrow path between the garden and the riding ring, where two women on horseback stopped to gape at the sight of my father, naked but for his brown bikini, totter by with those long black plastic rods balanced across his shoulders.

~

BY THE time I was accepted at Clark University in Worcester, Dad had managed to put up his third and last building. Tumblebrook Farm, Home of the Gerbil, now occupied 7,300 square feet of building space, and Dad was indisputably a gerbil czar, the world's foremost expert on and largest supplier of Mongolian gerbils. He had an inventory of more than 8,700 gerbils, with 2,600 new gerbils being born on our farm every week.

Dad had outlasted and outsold his competitors. Thanks to the gerbils, he now had a swimming pool and a Lincoln Continental. He could even indulge in an antique coin collection.

The gerbils also paid most of my college tuition when I headed off to Worcester. To supplement the rest, I took a job as a waitress in Abdow's Big Boy Restaurant, a landmark in Worcester because of the chubby Big Boy statue out front. Big Boy was decked out in checked pants and an Elvis Presley hairdo, and he bore a giant hamburger aloft like the Olympic torch. I made good money there because Abdow's was a home away from home for most of the city's drunks; once, a man handed me a fifty-dollar tip for spraying extra whipped cream onto his strawberry pie.

The running joke, whenever I came home from college, was to ask if we were rich enough yet for me to quit waitressing. Dad always shook his head and told me that we were still waiting for our ship to come in.

One weekend, though, he had a different answer. I came into the kitchen and found Mom frying chicken for dinner and Dad seated at the claw-footed oak table with a tumbler of scotch at his elbow. At the sight of me, Max the parrot cocked his head and scoffed like a Russian villain in a James Bond movie.

"Ah ha!" Max cried. "Ah ha ha ha!"

"Hey, Max," I said. "How are you?"

"Ah *ha*!" Max screeched even louder.

Dad rolled his eyes. "If we're lucky, that bird will die a timely but painless death while we're on vacation."

"You're going on vacation?" I was so surprised that I stopped in the middle of the kitchen and dropped my bags where I stood. It was a well-known fact that my parents never went anywhere.

"We all are," Dad said. "We need to do something as a family."

"But why? We never have before."

"It's a celebration." Dad picked up his scotch and held it up to the light for a minute, turning the glass in his hand. "This year, I made as much money as the governor of Massachusetts. What do you think of that?"

I sat down. "Wow." Max squawked and tried to bite my shoulder through the cage. I moved out of his reach. "That's great, Dad."

"Of course, the governor enjoys a few more perks than I do," Dad added generously. "A mansion. A staff. A secretary. A car at his disposal, and so forth."

"Still," I said. "That's quite an accomplishment. You must have sold a ton of gerbils."

"And you do have a secretary," Mom said, leaving the stove to come over to the table. "My mother's right upstairs." She sat down with us and reached for Dad's cigarettes. He tried to slide the package back into his pocket, but she was too quick for him.

"You'll have to take time off from your job," Dad informed me.

"How much time?"

"Two weeks, starting the Fourth of July."

I shook my head. "I can't do that," I said. "They count on me. And summer's the busiest season for tips. I need the money."

"You have to come with us," Mom said. She thought for a minute, and then added, "Of course, depending on where your father decides to take us, I might stay home, too."

"That's not an option," Dad said. "You both have to go on vacation. And that's an order," he added, smiling.

"But I'll get fired!" I protested. "Waitresses don't ever get vacations. Besides, I just barely memorized the prices on the menu and learned how to carry six hot plates without a tray."

"All useful skills, I'm sure," Mom said.

"Quit your job," Dad suggested. "That way they can't fire you."

I didn't quit, but I lied. When I went back to work that Sunday, I told the manager, a scrawny woman whose white hair net hung like a cobweb over her ears, that my little brother Phil had a life-threatening blood disease and would probably be dead by summer's end.

"My family needs me to spend time with them," I said. "Two weeks."

The manager sighed, unimpressed. "Call me if your brother doesn't die," she said. "I'll put you back on the schedule."

~

FOR our first and only family vacation, Dad couldn't bring himself to pay for a motel despite his governor's salary. Instead, he called us outside early on the day of our departure and said, "Surprise! We're traveling in style!"

An RV was parked in our driveway, the sort of camper that's one step up from a plumber's truck, with a bed over the cab and built-in furniture designed for leprechauns.

"It'll make Phil happy," Dad said as Mom, Donald, and I squinted in disbelief at the refrigerator on wheels that he assured us would sleep eight to ten people. "You know how crazy he is about campers. I told Phil that this is his birthday present. And there's room enough for each of you to bring a friend."

"Maybe if we tie our friends to the roof," Donald said.

Phil popped out of the RV door just then, banging metal against metal. "There's a bed over the steering wheel!" he yelled. "Can you believe it?" He was turning eight years old that August and was easily entertained.

"I am not going anywhere in that tin can," Mom announced.

"Oh, come on, Sally," Dad said. "Where's your sense of adventure? This camper has a fully equipped kitchen!"

"Exactly my point." Mom sniffed. "Camping is all about chores. And we know who does the chores around here." She turned around and started walking back toward the house. "You go," she called over one shoulder. "Take the kids with you. Now, that's what I'd call a vacation."

Mom hid in the house while we helped Dad load up the camper with canned goods, linens, clothes, more canned goods, a TV, and a grill. We had enough Dinty Moore canned beef stew to feed a ship full of Navy men.

Eventually, Dad went inside "to have a little talk with your mother." Phil climbed back into the camper to line up his stuffed animals on the bed above the cab while Donald and I lolled around on the grass, waiting for whatever would happen next.

Donald was easier to get along with since his near-death experience earlier that spring on a snake-hunting expedition to Belize. He'd driven to Central America in a caravan of high school students led by a guide with a guitar instead of a sense of direction. The guide had crashed their van into a truck full of rocks. While Donald's travel companions suffered from lacerations and broken bones, my brother was clever and agile enough to dive under the dashboard just before the accident; his only injuries were bruises in the shape of the radio knobs.

"Why do you think Dad's trying to make us all go on vacation?" I asked him now. "It's kind of weird, isn't it? Maybe he's having a midlife crisis."

"Nah. That was the Lincoln Continental," Donald said.

"Do you think he's feeling nostalgic because you're about to go to college?"

"The family is the pillar of society," Donald pronounced. "Ours might be a shaky pillar, but it's still standing. I think Dad's trying to save his marriage by taking a week off from the gerbils."

"He might as well have bought Mom another vacuum cleaner for her birthday, like last year," I said. "I can't believe he's going to try to put her in a camper."

"It's the Navy thing," Donald said confidently. "Dad just loves being shut up in a metal container. He can't understand why nobody else wants to be in there with him."

Eventually, Dad prevailed. Mom marched back outside, fiercely smoking a cigarette, her purse dangling over one arm. Dad followed. His face was paler than usual. Donald and I took one look at our parents and scrambled into the camper.

Our destination was Prince Edward Island, Canada, a road trip that would take us through New Hampshire, Maine, and New Brunswick. Our first stop was early that evening at a lake in New Hampshire, where Mom stood at the water's edge and refused to swim.

"See that?" she asked me, gesturing with her chin at the line of tubby women in sensible bathing suits standing waist deep in the water while their kids splashed around them like golden retrievers. "You know those women and kids are all peeing in the water. You might as well swim in a public toilet."

We drove another three hours north the next day to Popham Beach, Maine. The beach was cornbread gold and soft, and Donald and I dashed in and out of the waves with little Phil. I was surprisingly at peace. We must have looked like any other family, with our parents sitting in their webbed lounge chairs with the cooler between them while we swam.

However, all went sour the next night at our next campground, further north in Maine. There, ours was one of many RVs, and it was a tugboat amid cruise ships. Generators chugged and televisions blared all around us. You couldn't go to the showers without falling over people sprawled in webbed chairs with flesh hanging in pink bunches wherever it escaped from bathing suits and shorts.

"They're in a different class of people, campers," Mom said as we picked our way through the bodies.

That night, Mom started picking fights with Dad. It was over small things at first—she wanted to sleep alone in the bed above the cab and let Phil sleep with Dad—and escalated from there. Listening to them bicker, I realized that this was the longest time our family had ever been together, sleeping and eating in gerbilly close quarters, with no sprawling farm fields, animals, or chores to buffer us from one another.

Donald tried hard to entertain us that night with imitations of Uri Geller, the handsome Israeli who had laid claim to paranormal abilities such as telekinesis and telepathy. Geller had explained to the world that his special gifts were granted to him as a child when he was playing in a garden and struck by a strange light; he was best known for bending spoons with his mind.

As Donald laid out a row of plastic spoons on the picnic

table, we gathered around to watch. Donald stared hard at the utensils for several long, breathless moments, during which I nearly believed he could bend them. At last, though, he hit the spoons with his fist and sent them flying. "I can't be expected to bend plastic!" he said. "Show me some metal!"

Mom sighed. "You know, I'd really rather watch you shuck this corn with your mind than bend spoons."

"Yes. Plastic spoons aren't cheap, you know," Dad said, bending over to collect them from the pine needles around the rock so that he could wash them and stow the spoons in the camper again. "It's not like plastic spoons grow on trees."

Donald and I had a fit over that one, giggling so hard that Dad sent us out for more firewood. Later, as we fed the wood into the fire, our parents had their final argument. This one was about lobsters.

"All I want," Mom told my father, "is for you to indulge me just this once. I want you to drive down the street and buy a couple of lobsters." She set a giant pot of water over our puny campfire. "It'll take me that long to boil the damn water anyway."

"Please be quiet, Sally. People will hear you." Dad peered around at the other campers. There were so many campfires going that the whole forest looked ablaze.

"Nobody can hear me," Mom said. "Not over their *god-damn generators,*" she shouted, glaring at Dad. Mom was in full fighter stance now, head thrown back, both hands on her hips, her dark curls bouncing even while she stood still. "All I want is a lobster, and then I can die happy."

"We've got plenty to eat right here in the camper," Dad protested. "And it's too much work."

Mom snorted. "Like you've done any work around here."

"Sally, please lower your voice," Dad said. "Lobsters are too expensive."

"I bet they're not too expensive for the governor of Massachusetts," Mom said.

"If you don't want Dinty Moore's beef stew, we've got canned hash and soup," Dad said, sounding a little desperate. "And hot dogs! We've got plenty of hot dogs, Sally. Nobody even has to cook."

Mom shook her head at him, slipped on her big checkered oven mitts, picked up the pot of hot water, and doused the fire. "You're right. Nobody has to cook because I quit. I've tried camping and now I want to go home. If you won't take me, I'll find a bus."

And so, three days into our two-week vacation, we drove home in silence except for Phil crying "Uno!" every time I let him win at his card game at the little folding table in the back of the camper.

Chapter Nineteen

The Gerbil Czar Retires

The ark

CREDIT: THE HOLLY ROBINSON COLLECTION

At Clark University, I declared

biology as my major and won Dad's approval. Whenever anyone asked what I planned to do after graduation, I answered "med school" in the breezy manner of the wholly undecided.

In truth, I had little interest or talent in biology. The courses seemed like they should be interesting—biology was the very stuff of life, was it not?—but the lectures dragged on. My classmates were hell bent on getting into medical school. They took their class notes everywhere, even to the beach, and wouldn't attend a party until their lab reports were done. Even the textbooks bored me—an amazing thing, considering that I was such a voracious reader that I found delight in reading cereal boxes. My cell biology textbooks were filled with words as long as my arm, each one meaning something like "the kind of cell that has little hairs all over it."

I did reasonably well in my cell biology class at Clark junior year only because my best friend—a broad-shouldered smoker, an ex-alcoholic at the age of twenty-one who sauntered about campus in red sneakers—really *was* determined to make it into medical school. Louisa asked me to help her study with flash cards, so I learned the material by default.

My organic chemistry class was even worse than cell biology. The big-bellied, frog-eyed professor was often struck completely dumb by the presence, in the front row of this class, of a coed from New York who wore short skirts and deliberately lined up her colored pens between her legs, squeezing her thighs to hold them in place. At some point in every lecture you could count on her uncrossing her legs, allowing the pens to spill in all directions like a porcupine losing its quills.

I had never been so uninterested in school. Yet when my cell biology professor offered me a job in his laboratory, I jumped at the chance. It was time to move on from waitressing, I reasoned, and working as a lab assistant was one step closer to my ultimate goal of getting through medical school and saving the world in some as yet vague way. (In my fantasies, I lived in a thatch-roofed village, surrounded by children who narrowly escaped terminal illnesses because I had arrived with the right medicine in the nick of time; I had a great tan and dressed in those khaki vests that are mostly pockets.)

Dr. Cortina, my cell biology professor, wore white lab coats that were as clean and crisp as restaurant tablecloths before the appetizers. He provided me with my own lab coat, a little long in the sleeves, and told me that I could do anything I liked in the lab: play music, eat lunch, take a nap. "The nice thing about being a research scientist," he said, "is that you work your own hours. A lot of hours, but your own."

I stopped just short of telling him that I knew something about that, having lived with my father, and asked what kind of research I would be working on.

"Cancer," Dr. Cortina said. "We're studying how tumors grow."

Cancer! This was even better than anything I'd dreamed up in my fantasy life. Here was a chance to save millions! I followed Dr. Cortina out of his office, a small room dedicated to bookshelves and stacks of papers with mile-long titles, and down the hall to his laboratory. Dr. Cortina sat me down at a gray-speckled lab bench and brought something over on a tray. He set the tray in front of me and I nearly vomited.

It was a rat. I'd dissected animals in various classes, of course, but this rat wasn't like the neatly pickled, plastic-looking frogs and pigs I'd taken apart before. This rat was freshly killed, its fur still sleek and white, its snout a bright pink.

"As you can see, I've just split the belly open," Dr. Cortina was saying, pointing at the incision with one well-manicured finger. "You don't really need to make the incision this long, but it might make the work easier for you. And we'll just be discarding the rest of the rat when you're finished."

I nodded, biting my bottom lip. I could do this. Of course I could. This was what good scientists did, the basic research necessary to save the world from plagues, viruses, limps, and blindness.

"What do you want me to do after the rats are cut open?" I asked.

Dr. Cortina showed me how to remove the rat's ovaries—they looked like gray, evil-smelling grapes—and asked me to weigh them and record the weight in a particular column on a chart. He was testing a certain tumor-inhibiting chemical, he said, and the point was to see if it had worked. The rats we were dissecting all had ovarian tumors he'd induced to grow in them; by weighing the ovaries, he could calculate how and why the cancer had progressed or halted after the tumor-inhibiting medication.

And so that was my job, and I did it for three hours a day between classes. I played music to distract myself from thinking about what the rats had actually gone through, and I even developed enough of a stomach for the job that I could eat lunch at the same bench where I was about to split a rat open and remove her ovaries. I also became convinced that at some point in the afterlife someone was going to remove my ovaries and weigh them, because I believed in karma as much as I believed in anything.

When I called home to tell my parents that I'd given up my waitressing job at Big Boy, Dad was ecstatic about my new position as lab assistant. "Now you're really learning the scientific method," he enthused. "There are some things you can't learn in a textbook, and being meticulous in a laboratory is one of them."

"I don't know, Dad," I sighed. "This doesn't really feel right to me. Maybe I'm not cut out for med school."

"Of course you are!" he said. "I used to think I wanted you to take over the gerbil business. But you'll want a husband and a family one day, and becoming a doctor is a more viable career option." He sighed. "I make good money, but at what cost? If you're a do-it-yourself kind of person like me, there are obvious disadvantages. At least doctors can take vacations."

~

To my father's delight, his article "Gerbil or Jird: Seeking a Common Language for Biomedical Research" earned the most prominent headline on the cover of the September/October issue of *Lab Animal* magazine in 1975. The appearance of the article led him to ask if I could help out at the annual meeting of the American Association for Laboratory Animal Sciences. The conference was going to be held in Boston, he pointed out, at the Hynes Convention Center, so I wouldn't have to travel far from my apartment near Clark.

"This will be a watershed conference for me," Dad said. "I'm leading a panel seminar. You can work the booth while I'm in the seminar, maybe make a few career contacts," he urged. "You never know who's going to turn up at these meetings."

I made my way into Boston in my old white Galaxy Ford, got a badge at the door, and showed up at my father's booth. The Hynes Convention Center was an enormous, echoing space downtown. It was packed with animal breeders, researchers, clinicians, and vendors selling their cutting-edge laboratory animal equipment, like shields that would allow scientists to deliver germ-free rodents by cesarean section and pass them through to a foster nursing mother. None of the animals were present, but their pictures were everywhere, like pin-up posters: exotics such as nude mice and lemurs, and commonplace rats, rabbits, mice, and hamsters.

I found Dad at one of the cheap outer booths—you paid according to the size and location—and he looked dapper in a shirt and tie ordered from the Sears catalog for this very day. He'd dressed up his booth in Navy colors, blue and gold and white, and he had poster displays of gerbils. He was damp-palmed over the whole ordeal and pumped my hand as if I were a colleague.

"Your job is to man the booth while I give my talk," Dad said, eyeing my jeans and T-shirt. "I'm leading a panel seminar, 'The Gerbil in Research,' for three hours, starting at one o'clock."

"That's fine, Dad," I reassured him. "All I have to do is hand out these pamphlets about Tumblebrook Farm, right? And maybe some issues of the *Gerbil Digest*?"

He held up a hand in warning. "Not too many. It's expensive to print things these days. I wouldn't want to waste money on casual curiosity seekers."

"I don't see many of those here, Dad," I said. "I don't think you have to worry."

But telling my father not to worry was like telling him not to breathe. He had a "prestigious lady researcher from NIH" coming to talk about the brain research she was doing on gerbils, Dad informed me. "It should be a pretty good-sized crowd," he said nervously.

For his sake, I hoped so. I patted him on one broad shoulder and sent him on his way. "Go get 'em, Dad."

While he was gone, I defended myself against various salesmen interested in selling me equipment and immersed myself in a novel, occasionally handing out pamphlets to people who asked for them. In the booth next to ours, a film repeated over and over, announcing the benefits of a certain genetic strain of mice.

At last Dad returned, looking triumphant. "It went well, I take it," I said.

"You bet. We had over a hundred people. And that's not all." Dad leaned forward to whisper. "I finally met Henry Foster."

I had no idea who this was. "Is that good?"

"Is that good?" Dad laughed. "Of course it is. Henry Foster is the president of Charles River Laboratories, the world's largest supplier of mice and rats. He's a legend in his own lifetime!"

My father sat down on one of the little metal folding chairs he'd brought with him—he had a stack of these rescued from the dump and stored in our basement for just such an occasion—and reclined with his hands behind his head. Dr. Henry Foster was a veterinarian, Dad explained, who'd been struck by the same vision as Victor Schwentker: to provide clean, healthy rodents to academic researchers and scientists at drug companies. Foster first began breeding animals in a warehouse west of Boston, where he developed "pathogen-free rats," an essential step forward in laboratory animal science. The original company moved to a headquarters in Wilmington, Massachusetts, and had expanded to become Charles River Laboratories International, a conglomerate of over a hundred facilities and 8,400 employees in twenty different countries.

"You want to know the most amazing thing?" Dad asked.

"What's that?"

"Henry Foster is one of the ten richest men in Boston. But when I introduced myself to him, Henry Foster said, 'I know who you are.' Henry Foster knew all about my gerbils."

"That's great, Dad." I was honestly impressed.

My father nodded, smiling broadly, then quickly recovered his frown. "Of course, it never pays to take things for granted. I can't rest on my laurels."

~

I LASTED at my research job with Dr. Cortina for three months. Each week it grew more difficult to go. I was having headaches, which I blamed on the lab chemicals. I was sleep-deprived from trying to keep up with organic chemistry, which required hours in the laboratory as well as lectures and outside assignments, and from getting up every morning at 5:00 A.M. to work out with the crew team, which had replaced horseback riding as my obsession in Worcester. Dr. Cortina was overly understanding anytime I called to say I couldn't come in; he sweetly suggested that I "rest up" and come in when I could. "The work will still be here for you," he said.

Finally, one spring morning when the magnolia trees on Clark's campus were at their most delicate pink and the forsythia was so bright yellow that it made me blink, I went to work, sat at the lab bench in front of a rat turned belly-up on the dissecting tray, and realized I couldn't cut the rat open.

I didn't want to feel a rat's cold skin bristling with hairs beneath my hand as I pressed the animal into place. Not just today, but not ever again. I didn't want to be a doctor. I didn't want to have anything to do with a career that would require me to dissect animals. Even opening up the horseshoe crabs in my physiology class had made me sick to my stomach, and surely medical school would require worse things.

I tried hard to talk myself into staying on that bench in Dr. Cortina's lab. This was cancer, I reminded myself: public enemy number one. This was the work of the noble scientist. I was paving the way toward a cure. For every second that went by without me cutting open this animal, cancer was getting a leg up on humankind.

Dad was so proud whenever he told people that I was going to become a doctor. My father had devoted his life to raising gerbils as laboratory animals because it was a cause that he believed could make the world a better place. He wanted his children to live their lives with the same degree of passion and commitment to humanity. If I gave up here, if I told my father that I no longer wanted to study medicine or do medical research, he would be crushed.

I even tried speaking to myself in my father's voice, closing the door so that I could say the words aloud, like God lecturing Noah. "Focus, Holly," I boomed. "Focus on what's important. You are a servant of medicine."

But, in the end, nothing I said in my tortured monologue could make me pick up that knife. I finally put my tools away, slid the rat into the lab refrigerator, and made my way to Dr. Cortina's office, shoulders hunched, sneakers squeaking on the linoleum.

I found Dr. Cortina hunched between two towers of papers, scribbling something on a graph, concentrating so hard that the pink tip of his tongue was pinched between his teeth. He didn't hear me knock the first time.

"I don't think I can work for you anymore," I said when Dr. Cortina finally noticed me. "I'm sorry. Maybe I'm just not a biologist at heart."

"Really? But you do such good work in the lab." Dr. Cortina looked up at me from his desk with a kind smile. "Ah, well. So it goes." He seemed not the least bit rattled that I was quitting; of course, there were probably dozens of pre-meds coveting my place at his lab bench.

"I don't think that being careful in a laboratory is the same thing as being a scientist," I said. "Or a doctor."

"No, but it's a start." Dr. Cortina tapped his pen against one of the stacks of paper in front of him. "So what do you think you'll do, then? Are you going to change majors?"

"I don't know," I said.

"Do you like biology?"

I sighed. "Not really."

Dr. Cortina laughed and removed his glasses to wipe his eyes. "Then I think it's safe to conclude that science probably isn't your life's work," he said gently, donning his glasses again. "But don't despair. Better to find this out now than later. Too many people force themselves forward on a certain path because it's what they think they should do. Life's too short for that. Just keep asking yourself what makes you happy."

~

AFTER more teacher conferences where it was clear that nobody at the local high school knew what to do with my brother Philip, Mom and Dad finally put my little brother in a private school in Worcester, "a place where at least the teachers are smarter than he is," Mom said. Occasionally, when it was Mom's turn to drive the car pool, she would stop by to take me to lunch.

Two months after I left my laboratory job and returned to Big Boy—a move I still hadn't confessed to my parents—my mother called to say that she was coming to see me. I went to my morning classes and headed home to clean the apartment. I was living with vegetarian roommates; one of them, Vicki, was seated at the kitchen table when I came home, wearing a pair of enormous sunglasses and slicing up raw steak.

"What are you doing?" I asked. "Why are you wearing sunglasses indoors?"

"It's the flesh," she said, gesturing at the bloodied beef strips on the table. "I'm cooking for Harry tonight, and I wanted to surprise him by fixing his birthday dinner here. He said he wanted a real he-man, red-meat meal. But I can't stand the sight of this poor wounded flesh."

"Oh. Okay. Listen, my mom's coming over. Do you think you could clean up some of that blood before she gets here?"

Vicki nodded and went back to her dramatic carving while I made my bed and stood in the hallway, wondering what to do about the clay. Leaving my job in Dr. Cortina's lab had left me with free time during the day, since I mostly waitressed at night; I had signed up for pottery classes on a whim. The act of centering a lump of clay on a spinning wheel and transforming it between my hands, shaping a vase, pitcher, or bowl, absorbed me like nothing else I'd ever tried.

I'd prevailed upon Donald to come and help me build my own pottery wheel from a kit. He'd agreed because I paid him, and because it involved pouring a cement flywheel. I had put the wheel in an alcove in the hallway and lined the walls and floor with plastic, but I still managed to splatter raw clay everywhere.

My roommates didn't mind traipsing through clay to get to their bedrooms, but now that I was faced with trying to clean, I realized it was like the Dr. Seuss book *The Cat in the Hat:* like the cat spreading the pink spot that he wants to remove, anything I used to clean up the clay just transferred the clay to the next surface I touched.

I tried to meet my mother downstairs when she arrived, but she was too quick for me. She came through the kitchen and stopped at the hallway threshold to stare at the clay, the pottery wheel, and the shelves of greenware I'd been drying before taking them over to Clark to fire in the kiln.

"What on earth is all this?" she asked.

"A pottery wheel," I said.

She gave me a look. "Please don't tell me that this is your mess."

"Okay."

Mom sighed. "I hope your landlord doesn't pay you a surprise visit."

We went out to lunch and then stopped at the grocery store, as always, where Mom tried to convince me to let her buy me more food than I needed. "My roommates are vegetarians," I explained. "I really just need rice and beans."

She dismissed this. "We're not living in Mexico, you know."

As we shopped for food, I finally told Mom about my decision to stop working in Dr. Cortina's laboratory.

"Well, that's too bad," she said. "You know how your father worries about your lack of focus. But you'll still get your degree in biology, won't you? It seems too late to change majors at this point, with just one year to go."

I nodded. "Yes. But I want to be an artist instead of a doctor."

We were walking back to the car. Mom stopped and turned to glare at me. "You'll end up living on cat food if you're an artist," she said. "Why don't you go to nursing school?"

"I can't work at a job I don't love," I said firmly.

"I knew it was a mistake to send you to such a liberal college," Mom said. "Look, you can't be a debutante all your life. There may come a day when you have to buy your own groceries."

We rode home in silence, my throat thick with anger. What had my mother done with her life but mooch off Dad? Immediately, though, I knew this was unfair: my mother had followed her own bliss, working hard to run a riding stable that barely made ends meet and devoting her life to caring for us. So I said nothing.

Mom parked the station wagon on the street below my apartment building and we began hauling the bags of groceries up the open back staircase. I lived on the second floor; as I fumbled with keys to unlock the door, we both happened to glance down at the car from the back porch. A tall, skinny man with a blue shirt that hung on him like a flag on a pole was sauntering up to the open tailgate of Mom's station wagon. He glanced around and then began gathering up the remaining bags of groceries as if they belonged to him.

"He can't do that!" Mom cried indignantly. "I paid good money for that food!"

"He just did, though," I said, laughing a little as the thief began sauntering up the street. He might as well have been whistling. "Look, if he's that hungry, he probably deserves the food more than I do."

"The hell with that," Mom said.

Before I could stop her, Mom ran down the two flights of stairs. I watched in astonishment from the back porch as my nimble mother, looking very small from my vantage point, trotted up behind the man and started whaling away at him with her purse. Before I could make it down the stairs, the man had dropped the bags and run.

I helped Mom collect the scattered groceries. "I'm not sure if that was brave or stupid," I said. "But it was amazing."

Mom balanced a bag of groceries on one hip. "We work too hard for our money to let anyone steal from us," she said with a sniff.

~

LATE one Friday night, I drove home from Clark for a weekend of spring trail riding. I spent the night in my old bedroom and looked out the window as soon as I woke up the next morning, excited to see the horses grazing in the pastures.

The horses were there. But there was something else, too, something that hadn't been there before: there was an ark in our yard.

I wandered down to the kitchen, where Mom was having her second cup of coffee after mucking out stalls, and pointed out the window. "What is that thing?"

"Oh, that's just your father's boat," she said. "It arrived early this morning."

I slipped into a pair of boots and went outside to walk around Dad's newest passion. The boat was a 1928 cabin cruiser, thirty-eight feet long and all wood and brass. The vessel was up on a stand, bringing it halfway up to the second-floor windows of our house.

Dad poked his head over the boat's bow railing and

grinned down at me. "You know, this was once a real pleasure cruiser," he told me. "This boat had her heyday on the Great Lakes."

"It looks like it would sink like a rock," I said.

Dad looked hurt. "Well, we *are* going to fix it up, you know."

And they did. My father and Donald worked on that boat all summer, hammering on new boards and caulking holes and seams, adding bits of brass scavenged from flea markets, and making the ark seaworthy.

For the boat's maiden voyage, Dad paid someone to trailer it two hours to the coast. He and Donald put the boat in the water in Scituate, Massachusetts, where Dad had found a prospective buyer. It took six bilge pumps to empty the boat of water once it was floating, since the shrinkage in the boards during the months the boat was on land had caused gaps between them.

Afterward, Donald called home to tell us about their journey. "Dad wanted to drive the boat," he said, laughing, "and we had to come into this pier with these big metal rings on the posts. I was up front with the ropes when Dad crashed the boat into the metal rings. Man, you crash fourteen tons of boat into metal, and the metal bends like a pretzel."

I winced. "Was anybody watching?"

"Oh, yeah," Donald said. "We came roaring in, and there was a whole crowd there. You should've heard them yelling when we cracked the dock."

I came home again a few weekends later and wandered out toward the stable after breakfast on Saturday morning. Dad was standing outside in the empty space on the lawn where his ark had been. He wasn't doing anything. He wasn't even smoking a cigarette.

"What are you doing out here, Dad?" I asked.

"Oh, just thinking."

"About what?"

My father glanced over his shoulder toward the gerbil buildings, barely visible behind the thick green foliage of the trees in full leaf. "Retirement."

"Really?" I folded my arms and studied my father more closely. He looked the same, dressed as always in stained khaki work pants—the bottom half of one of his old Navy uniforms—and an equally tired white T-shirt. He wore a blue duck-billed cap to keep the sun off his head, which was already peeling. Dad was still fit and square-shouldered and handsome, with a posture that suggested he was standing at attention. Pencils protruded from his pants pocket, along with the little spiral notebook full of lists he always carried.

"The business is almost ripe for selling," he explained. "We'll always have a conventional colony of gerbils. I don't have the ability, or the interest, to make the animals completely germ-free, and that's certainly what researchers are starting to want these days." He sighed. "I think I'll sell the business to Henry Foster. Charles River can certainly afford to buy me out."

"When?"

As always, when it came to talking about money, Dad was cagey. "We're just in the talking stages right now. It might take a few years. But I know they'll want to make a deal eventually. If Charles River can get their hands on my line of inbred gerbils, nobody else in the world will ever be able to compete with them." He turned his attention back to the lawn in front of us and fell silent again. The grass was slightly brown, still, where the boat had stood for so long.

"Are you really ready to retire, though?" I asked. "You're not that old."

"No," Dad said. "I'm not old yet." He offered me the ghost of a smile. "But I'm not young, either. I guess I'll have to find something else to do, now that the boat is gone and the gerbil business is pretty much running itself these days."

"Why did you get that boat, anyway?" I asked.

Dad looked at me for a long time, his blue eyes steady. "I don't know," he said. "What is it about having a boat? It's all about going after a dream, I guess."

I nodded and stood there with my father for a while longer, staring at the empty space where the boat had been, picturing the polished wood and gleaming brass, and all of the places a boat like that could take you.

Epilogue

The American Gerbil Show

It takes me half an hour to drive down to the sixth annual American Gerbil Society gerbil show in Bedford, Massachusetts. The show is being held at the Bedford Plaza, a modest three-story brick hotel with a swimming pool, a restaurant, and free pitchers of iced tea and lemonade in the lobby. There is no outward sign that the hotel has been overrun by gerbil enthusiasts from as far away as Missouri and Oregon, Canada and Argentina, other than the nervous desk clerks who eye people's pockets as if expecting rodents to pop right out of them.

I've brought my son, Aidan, and two of his friends with me. The boys charge up the three flights of stairs to the conference room, which is packed with more than a hundred people. A spillover crowd mills around outside the doors. Rows of tables line the room, with more tables in the center. The tables are piled with cages brought in by breeders who are showing off not only gerbils but other exotic pocket pets as well: dwarf hamsters and South African pygmy hedgehogs, ferrets and degus, chinchillas, and pygmy mice no bigger than my fingernail.

As I mingle with members of the American Gerbil Society, I recall one of my mother's favorite sayings: "There's a lid for every pot." The breeders are all earnest and friendly. They are the sorts of people who wear their many passions emblazoned on their T-shirts: American Gerbil Society, Greyhound Festival, Christmas Revels, Audubon Society. If they weren't here, these people would be out walking for good causes.

"Pygmy mice babies are so small that you have to be careful not to dump the little ones out when you change the shavings," one breeder tells Aidan as my son watches her mini-mice nibble and hop.

"I probably shouldn't admit this here, but I've always liked hamsters better than gerbils," confides the solitary hamster breeder at the show, a redhead with a pierced tongue and a herd of plush black teddy bear hamsters. "It's a strictly aesthetic thing. I don't like rodents with tails."

One of the gerbil breeders proudly shows me her foundation sire, a marvelously muscular black-and-white pied gerbil alone in a cage. "I had him paired with a lovely Siamese girl, but I'm retiring him now," she explains when I ask where the gerbil's mate is. "He's going to live out the rest of his days with one of his grandsons."

A few side tables in the conference room display gerbil paraphernalia for sale: gerbil bags and gerbil hats, gerbil blankets and crazy-looking wooden gerbil houses, books about gerbils and statues of gerbils, too. One item for sale is a book about a gerbil who sculpts; the author, Judith Block, is a New York artist who has kept a tank of gerbils in her kitchen since 1972. She is petite with springy red curls and oversized glasses, and clearly in her element as she helps judge one of the pet classes. She once bought gerbils from my father, Judith tells me when I introduce myself.

"Gerbils are all about love," she says, handing a small plastic cage back to a pint-sized boy with freckles. "Gerbils are so intelligent and fun, and each one has a different personality." She gazes down at the boy, her eyes magnified, hypnotizing, and asks him what his gerbil does best.

"Nibbles!" the boy says. "That's his name, too."

The pet class begins as Judith and I talk. A teenage boy with an elaborate sound system and a smooth disc-jockey voice proclaims, "Lilac and Blossom can run on their wheel in tandem!" as their young owner holds up their carry cage for everyone to see. For the first time in decades, I remember Kinky, my unappreciated gerbil, born decades ahead of her time, and imagine myself here as a child, showing off her tricks. Where is that wrinkle in time when you need it most?

Meanwhile, Judith tells me that her favorite pet of all time was Phoebe, a gerbil artist whose work was so phenomenal that Judith created not only the book on display here but also a website to showcase it: www.phoebe.agsgerbils.org. In the preface of her webpages, Judith calls the sculptures crafted by Phoebe the gerbil "reminiscent of certain species of cactus, or of archeological finds in the Bayanzag Valley of the Gobi Desert, where some of the world's oldest dinosaur fossils have been discovered. Since Phoebe, born in NYC, has never left the Riverdale section of the Bronx, her works perhaps harken back to DNA memory, or possibly to some interspecies, Jungian collective unconscious."

Phoebe's sculptures appear on the website with titles such as *Twilight on the Gobi, Antler Totem,* or *Desert Cloud.* Judith has written a haiku for each of them, and the haiku appears in Spanish as well as English, thanks to an Argentine gerbil lover, Laura Pimás, whom Judith met through the American Gerbil Society. For instance, the haiku for *Twilight on the Gobi* reads:

The violet hour.
The long, hot day is over.
I love the cold night.

La hora purpura.
El ardiente, largo día ha terminado.
Amo la fría noche.

"Phoebe was unique," Judith concludes fondly. "All gerbils chew cardboard tubes and destroy them, but Phoebe was an artist in a gerbil's body. She'd chew on a colored cardboard tube, then step away and look at what she'd done, and then go back and chew, just like an artist who never thinks her art is finished. If her sculptures were done by people and brought to a design class, we'd say they're works of art."

In the next room, judges in white coats prod and examine and play with various gerbils competing in their show classes, evaluating them for body build, color, and personality in much the same way judges examine dogs at the Westminster Dog Show. Males are supposed to be buff, females more streamlined, and all prize-winning gerbils have fur tails with admirable tufts. A gerbil's biggest dream, or at least his owner's, is to win Best in Show.

The gerbils at the American Gerbil Society show look nothing like my dad's. Ours were plain brown, with black tufts on their tails and creamy bellies. Here, there are orange gerbils with white bellies and ruby eyes. There are deep gray gerbils, light gray purplish gerbils, and nutmeg gerbils—that's a calico color. There are even Siamese gerbils that look just like Siamese cats, except that they're gerbils.

I stand around and watch the judging for a bit. "Every gerbil at an AGS show is handled by a judge," says American Gerbil Society president Donna Anastasi, one of the show judges and author of the top-selling gerbil book for pet lovers, *Gerbils: The Complete Guide to Gerbil Care* (Bowtie, 2005). "If they nip, they lose points on personality. At hamster shows, the judges don't even handle the animals," she adds with a sniff. "They have to pick the hamsters up with a scoop."

Donna is a young, fit-looking mother of two, a soccer mom married to a college professor. She graduated from Smith College and now works as a human-factors engineer. "Go ahead and call me nerdy," she laughs. "I definitely am."

As we chat, there is an instant connection. Like me, Donna is the daughter of a military man; children who grow up with Air Force, Army, or Navy parents have a special radar for one another, perhaps because we're always friendly but hold a part of ourselves in reserve. We know from experience that you can lose everything you hold dear in an instant.

Donna's father was a lieutenant colonel in the Air Force, and she attended eight different schools before he retired. "I was shy to begin with, so moving was really hard for me," she confesses.

She attributes her passion for animals to that Air Force upbringing. "It took years of begging to get one parakeet because we moved around so much." In 1999, she bought her first gerbils at a pet store on a whim, "for the kids."

Today, Donna is a gerbil guru. Her website, ABC Gerbils, earns hundreds of hits daily. Through the years she has bred for gentle temperament and special colors, and to eliminate seizures and other common, naturally occurring health problems in gerbils. Her latest mission is to acquire a blue gerbil; she's excited because a gerbil-loving buddy of hers who is traveling to Iraq has promised to bring her one.

"We don't have any blue gerbils in the States yet," she says. "They have them in Europe, but they aren't willing to give them up." She laughs. "European gerbil societies, like the National Gerbil Society in Britain, think that Americans jump into things too quickly. Like, we've already made 'mottled' an official color category, but that's still provisional for them. The British gerbil breeders seem to think that we Americans are loose cannons."

~

THE world of gerbil fanciers is underground unless you look for it, a mostly online community that gathers twice a year for shows. The American Gerbil Society didn't exist when Dad started his farm, but many of its members have heard of him.

My father ended up selling his inbred line of Tumblebrook Farm gerbils to Charles River Laboratories, which continues to provide them to scientists around the world for research studies. Charles River is the Microsoft of laboratory animal companies; these days it's headed up by Jim Foster, Henry's son, named "Entrepreneur of the Year" by *Forbes* magazine in 2002, the same year that Charles River was named "Company of the Year" by the *Boston Globe*.

Jim led the company's foray into providing preclinical testing services for pharmaceutical companies, recognizing that with new techniques using computer models and cell cultures, the need for disease research on live animals is rapidly diminishing. In the past five years, Charles River's laboratory animal business has declined from 80 percent of its profits to just 40 percent.

Terrence Fisher, the man who sealed the original deal with Dad, agreed to meet with me last year when I called and expressed curiosity about where our gerbils had ended up. I drove to the main headquarters of Charles River in Wilmington, Massachusetts. Fisher, the general manager of business development and surgical services for North American research models, is a small man but moves like a professional athlete. He bounces on the balls of his feet with his shoulders thrown back; when it emerged later that he was in the military until joining Charles River in 1979, I wasn't surprised.

My father's gerbils—or rather, a germ-free line of their descendants—are housed not in Wilmington but in a separate facility in Kingston, New York, because of government regulations. But Fisher gave me a tour of one of the animal buildings, and I breathed in the familiar pungent smells of rodents, wood shavings, and food pellets. The food and water bottles looked just like ours. So did the racks of clear cages with wire tops.

On closer inspection, though, Charles River is a completely

different kind of laboratory animal facility. Tumblebrook Farm was mostly a family business, a farm of sorts. We often had gerbils running loose; curious escapees would come and sit on my foot while I was cleaning cages, and I'd scoop them up and toss them back into a cage. Our workers were spotty sweepers, too, so there was always a scattering of shavings and pellets on the floor.

The Charles River floors are freshly painted and surgically clean, even with more than 187,000 mice and rats living in the one building I saw. The food at Charles River is irradiated and then placed into vacuum-sealed bags to keep it free of contaminants. The air the animals breathe is filtered. So is the water they drink. The rodents are housed in isolation tanks—separate rooms within the larger building that are created by plastic walls, with perhaps two dozen cages in each. The workers wear surgical scrubs and never come into skin-to-skin contact with their rodent charges.

To do anything with the animals, the caretakers have to insert their arms into giant plastic sleeves built into isolation tank walls and attached to unnervingly bright green gloves. As an added precaution against disease, Charles River inserts "nude sentinels" into the colonies. These are rodents with no immune systems who act like canaries in a coal mine.

Because the isolator tanks at Charles River are pressurized, occasionally the plastic sleeves and gloves pop out of them when they're not in use and they start waving about in the aisles like ghosts. The workers must be used to this strange sight, but I walked carefully down the center of every aisle behind Terrence Fisher, not wanting to feel those cold green plastic fingers on my face or shoulder. There was something too cold and sterile about it all; I couldn't even imagine holding one of these mice. Maybe, for the workers, that made their jobs easier, I thought: not being able to feel the warmth of the animals in their hands.

As Fisher walked me to the door of the building, a sudden rain shower sent sheets of water across the parking lot. We stood around for a while beneath the awning, waiting for the rain to let up, and I asked Fisher if he remembered meeting my father.

"Of course," he said. "I went out to Tumblebrook Farm several times. That was quite a place you people had."

"What was my dad like?"

Fisher's answer surprised me. "He was a very soft-spoken man," he said. "Very gentle and never in a hurry."

"Do you remember anything else about him?"

Fisher grinned. "That man was absolutely in love with gerbils," he said. "I don't think I've ever seen a man so immersed in his work."

"Oh, yes," I said. "That's my dad."

~

OUR family, like so many, is separated by geography now. My brother Philip studied Russian history, stopping just short of a doctorate. He now works at a large university, happily managing other people's websites while dabbling in passions that range from playing the banjo to parsing sentences in Old Norse.

My brother Donald moved to England for a job twenty years ago and is there still with his wife and two daughters. Contrary to all of our worst predictions for his future, Donald managed to make it through technical college studying biomedical engineering and, through sheer grit, intelligence, and energy, worked his way up to the post of sales director for a large software company. His territory now covers central Europe, and he makes so much money that he can say, with authority, that the more degrees you earn from universities, the less money you're likely to make, holding my brother Phil and me up as prime examples. All three of us live in antique farmhouses.

Until his death on January 10, 2009, my father lived in South Carolina with my mother, in a modest brick ranch house across the street from an elementary school. They were divorced shortly before he sold Tumblebrook Farm to Charles River, when the cumulative stress of their twenty-eight-year marriage finally was too much to bear. They spent eighteen years apart, and my father was married to another woman for most of that time. Then, quite suddenly, Dad left his second wife and my parents decided to marry again.

"Better the devil you know," Mom says, summing up their situation.

Before his retirement from gerbil farming, Dad succeeded in accomplishing one last goal that was close to his heart: in 1987, he provided four pairs of his gerbils to Dr. Sigmund T. Rich in Los Angeles, the veterinarian who first encouraged my father to film gerbil seizures and write up his observations. Dr. Rich, whose life's work involved cataloging the many different strains of gerbils in China, hand-carried my dad's Tumblebrook Farm gerbils to Chinese researchers.

Afterward, Dr. Rich wrote to my father:

I want to thank you on behalf of our colleagues in China for your generous gift of four breeding pairs of your inbred strain. It gave me a very special feeling to have the historic role of bringing them back to their native homeland after 52 years in Japanese and American laboratories. (I estimate 150 to 200 generations!?)

~

HALFWAY into the afternoon at the American Gerbil Society show, there is an exciting announcement: "The Gerbil Olympics will begin in five minutes!"

Tension builds fast as entrants scurry to line up their cages along a row of tables by the windows. Each owner is given a small paper cup to hold over the cage. At the count of "One, two, three!" the cups are dropped into the cages. The gerbils start chewing with great zeal, whittling down the cups at an amazing speed. The winner is the gerbil able to demolish more paper cup than any other competitor in the span of two minutes. As I watch the gerbil contenders chew, I think about how much my father would have loved being here.

When Aidan and his friends are finally ready to leave the gerbil show, they run down the sidewalk to the parking lot ahead of me. As the boys buckle their seat belts in the car, they talk about the animals and which ones they'd like as pets.

Jack wants a ferret because he'd like to set up a little hammock for it next to his bed. Patrick longs for a miniature hedgehog because the ones we saw at the show burrowed under bits of cloth called "hedgehog hats" and walked around like fuzzy turtles. Aidan announces that he liked the dwarf hamsters best because he doesn't know anybody else who has them. He's already scheming, plotting out arguments that might convince his father and me to agree to let him breed a colony of dwarf hamsters in his room.

"I don't want a gerbil, because I already know a lot about those," he explains to his friends. "My grandfather used to raise them."

"How many gerbils did your grandfather have?" Jack wants to know.

I glance into the rearview mirror and meet Aidan's eyes. He grins at me. "Try to guess," he says.

Acknowledgments

THE author gratefully acknowledges the generous support of her agent, Richard Parks, the nicest man in New York, and of her friends, many of them writers and thoughtful critics despite the infinite demands of motherhood and jobs, especially Sharon Wright, Emily Ferrara, Susan Straight, Terri Giuliano Long, Elisabeth Brink, Virginia Smith, and Carla Panciera. I would also like to thank Jay Neugeboren, whose mentorship meant the world to me, and Lorraine Glennon, my first editor at *Ladies' Home Journal,* who taught me more about writing than any graduate school could. I would like to extend a heartfelt thank-you to Julia Pastore, too, my clever, visionary, and thorough editor who helps writers see that some books can, and should, take a completely different shape from what we first had in mind. Finally, many thanks to members of the American Gerbil Society, especially to Donna Anastasi and Judith Block, for their own dedication to the remarkable gerbil and for their help in writing this book.

About the Author

HOLLY ROBINSON has been a contributing editor at *Ladies' Home Journal* and *Parents* magazines, and her work has appeared in *American Baby, The Boston Globe, Family Circle, FamilyFun, Fitness, Good Housekeeping, More, Parenting, Shape,* and *WorkingMother.* She holds a B.A. in biology from Clark University and is a graduate of the M.F.A. program in creative writing at the University of Massachusetts, Amherst. In addition to her husband and their five children, she shares a home with two dogs, one cat, five fish, one gecko, and a Teddy Bear hamster. Visit her at AuthorHollyRobinson.com.